Reading
Skills Assessment

·····································

Teacher's Edition
Grade 4

D1240099

Senior Author

Dr. Roger C. Farr

Chancellor's Professor and Director of
the Center for Innovation in Assessment,
Indiana University, Bloomington

Harcourt

Orlando   Boston   Dallas   Chicago   San Diego

Visit *The Learning Site!*
www.harcourtschool.com

Printed in the United States of America

ISBN 0-15-312819-4

3 4 5 6 7 8 9 10 170 2003 2002 2001 2000

Table of Conte~~nts~~

Harcourt • Reading Skills Assessment

Appendix

· ·

Directions

Scoring/Interpreting

Annotated Facsimiles

Answer Keys

Harcourt • Reading Skills Assessment

iv   Teacher's Edition / Grade 4

Assessment and Evaluation in *Collections*

by Dr. Roger C. Farr

Knowing how well a student can use literacy skills such as reading, writing, listening, speaking, and viewing is vital to effective instruction.

Without the information provided by assessment, a teacher does not have a solid basis for planning instruction. This does not mean that teachers should constantly administer formal tests to students. Teacher observations, discussions with students, and a variety of informal assessments of all types are also important and valuable sources of information.

An assessment program should be integral to instruction. The Harcourt assessments have been carefully designed to provide teachers and schools with the information they need when they need it. The Harcourt assessments provide a comprehensive picture of students' achievement as they progress through the program. That picture provides the basis for school and classroom planning.

Formal and Informal Assessments

The Harcourt assessments include both informal and formal assessments. Informal assessments encourage teachers to observe students as they read, write, and discuss. These assessments provide immediate feedback and allow teachers to quickly determine which students are having difficulty and need additional practice.

Formal assessment is an opportunity for a teacher to take a more focused look at how students are developing their literacy skills. Some of the formal assessments, such as the *Reading Skills Assessment*, focus on whether students understand and apply the skills they have been taught by asking them to choose answers. Other assessments, such as the *Holistic Reading Assessment* and the *Reading/Writing Performance Assessment*, ask them to write either short or longer responses to what has been read or discussed. The formal assessments follow the formats used on many state and national standardized tests.

The *Portfolio Assessment Teacher's Guide* offers practical suggestions for using portfolios. Portfolios provide opportunities for students to collect samples of their reading and writing materials and to discuss their progress with teachers. Portfolios provide students with opportunities to reflect on their progress as readers and writers and to become effective self-assessors. Indeed, effective self-assessment should be the highest goal of an assessment program.

Collections Assessment Components

••

The chart below gives a brief overview of the assessment resources that are available in *Collections*.

Formal Assessments		
For placement and diagnosis	**Level**	**Purpose**
Kindergarten and Grade 1 Reading Inventory	K–1	To diagnose prerequisite literacy skills and assist in placement
Grades 2 and 3 Reading Inventory	2–3	To diagnose early literacy skills
Placement and Individual Inventory Teacher's Guide	2–6	To make placement decisions; to diagnose individual students
At the theme level		
Reading and Language Arts Skills Assessment *Reading Skills Assessment*	1 2–6	To measure progress; to diagnose skill competence
Holistic Reading Assessment	1–6	To obtain a global picture of reading comprehension
Reading/Writing Performance Assessment	1–6	To measure progress in reading comprehension and writing
At the selection level		
Selection Comprehension Tests	1–6	To monitor vocabulary and comprehension
Throughout the year		
Emergent Literacy in Kindergarten	K	To assess early literacy skills
Portfolio Assessment Teacher's Guide	1–6	To give teachers tips on starting, maintaining, and evaluating portfolios
At mid-year or end-of-year		
Mid-Year and End-of-Year Reading and Language Arts Skills Assessments	1	To provide a cumulative evaluation of skills development
Mid-Year and End-of-Year Reading Skills Assessments	2–6	To provide a cumulative evaluation of skills development

Informal Assessments
Teacher's Edition

◆ Assessment suggestions for each theme
◆ Assessment notes at "point of use" throughout the lessons
◆ Informal inventories/running records
   Grade 1: 2 per theme, 12 per grade
   Grades 2–6: 1 per theme, 6 per grade

◆ Writing Rubrics
◆ Self-assessment strategies

◆ Test Prep notes for skills lessons, writing, and grammar

Leveled Library (Primary/Intermediate Library)

◆ Benchmark Books for Evaluation

◆ Running records for trade books

General Assessment Considerations

Description of the Reading Skills Assessments

The *Reading Skills Assessments* are criterion-referenced tests designed to measure students' achievement on the skills taught in *Collections*. Criterion-referenced scores help teachers make decisions regarding the type of additional instruction that students may need.

Six *Reading Skills Assessments* are available at this grade level—one assessment for each theme at Grade 4. The assessments evaluate students' achievement in decoding, vocabulary, literary concepts, comprehension, and study and research skills. The formats used on the *Reading Skills Assessments* follow the style and format presented in the Teacher's Edition and *Practice Book*. This ensures that the student is presented with familiar formats on the assessment.

Scheduling the Assessments

The *Reading Skills Assessments* have been designed to correlate with specific skills introduced and reinforced within each theme of the program. Therefore, a *Reading Skills Assessment* could be administered as a pretest before a theme is started to determine which skills need to be emphasized. Or, a *Reading Skills Assessment* could be administered after a theme is completed to verify that students can apply the skills that were taught.

If possible, a *Reading Skills Assessment* should be given in one session. The pace at which you administer the tests will depend on your particular class and group. The tests are not timed. Most students should be able to complete an assessment in thirty to forty-five minutes.

Administering the Assessments

Accommodations can be made for students with special needs (e.g., special education, ESL). If accommodations are made for a student, they should be noted in the space provided on the cover of the assessment booklet.

Prior to administering a *Reading Skills Assessment*, the following general directions should be read to the students.

Say: *Today you will be answering questions about some of the things we have learned together in class. Do your very best and try to answer each of the questions.*

When administering the assessment, repeat or clarify items that students do not hear or directions that they do not understand, but do not permit such explanations to reveal any answers.

Specific Directions for Administering the Reading Skills Assessment

The directions for each assessment are printed on the pages of the student assessment booklets. There are no additional directions. If you wish, you may have students read the directions silently by themselves, or you may choose to read the directions aloud while students read them silently. Remember, if necessary, you may clarify any directions that students do not understand, as long as the clarification does not reveal any answers. Allow enough time for all students to complete the assessment or portion of the assessment being administered.

Scoring and Interpreting the Reading Skills Assessment

The *Reading Skills Assessment* can be scored in one of two ways. You may use either the annotated facsimile pages of the assessment booklets or the answer keys. Both can be found in this booklet. Follow these steps:

1. Open this booklet to the answer key or annotated facsimile page of the subtest to be scored.

2. Compare the student's responses, item by item, to the responses on the answer key and put a check mark next to each item that is correctly answered. It is recommended that you score the same subtest for all students before going on to score the next subtest. This method has been found to be more accurate and less time-consuming than scoring an entire assessment at one time.

3. Count the correct responses for the subtest and write this number on the Score line provided at the end of the subtest and on the booklet cover.

4. Continue this procedure for each subtest.

5. If you wish to evaluate a student's performance on a particular subskill, note on the cover of the test booklet which items measure that skill, and score that particular subskill. The number possible and the number needed to reach criterion are listed next to the line for the pupil score.

A student who scores at or above the criterion level for each subtest is considered competent in that skill area and is probably ready to move forward without additional practice. A column for writing comments about "Pupil Strength" has been provided on the cover of the assessment booklet.

A student who does not reach criterion level probably needs additional instruction and/or practice. See the "Reading Skill Prescriptions for Reteaching" section of this booklet for more information.

A student's score on each skill or objective is a good estimate of how that student would perform on all possible items related to that objective. Enter a student's scores for all subtests on the Student Record Form found in this booklet. Criterion-referenced test scores should provide information you can use to plan instruction. Examine the student's scores for each subtest and decide whether you should "Move Forward" or "Reteach." Place an **M** or **R** in the "Diagnostic Category" column to record your decision.

Move Forward means that the student has reached the criterion level for a skill, and reading instruction can move forward.

For example, on a subtest where there are 12 items, if the student scores 9 correct, and the criterion score for the subtest is 9/12, the student will receive **M** for **Move Forward.** This means that the student should be given practice in sustained reading to apply that particular reading skill. It does not mean that the student will never encounter any difficulty with that skill, nor does it mean that the skill is totally mastered. It does mean that the student seems to be quite good at that skill and should be given the opportunity to apply the skill to actual reading activities.

Reteach means that the student did not reach the criterion level for that skill. The student encountered difficulty with the skill and may have trouble understanding the skill. You should provide extra teaching on this skill with this student. The extra teaching may often be quite brief and may be accomplished through the skill prescriptions found in this booklet. Usually the student will need just a bit of extra guidance from you, accompanied by specific practice on the skill.

If a student scores at the **Reteach** level on only one of the test objectives, you may want to take the time to reteach that skill. The student may be grouped with other students who have experienced similar difficulty with that skill. However, when only one skill area is low, the student may have merely misunderstood the test directions or inadvertently forgotten to do several questions. If a student scores at the **Reteach** level on just one of the test objectives, the student should not have any great difficulty moving on to the next theme. If a student scored at the **Reteach** level on two objectives, the student should definitely be given extra help as he or she moves on to the next theme.

If a student scores at the **Reteach** level on more than two objectives, the student may need a considerable amount of extra help. Moving that student along without extra help might cause more problems, since the student is almost certain to encounter frustration in learning to read.

A *Reading Skills Assessment* is just one observation of a student's reading behavior. It should be combined with other evidence of a student's progress, such as the teacher's daily observations, student work samples, and individual reading conferences. The sum of all of this information, coupled with test scores, is more reliable and valid than any single piece of information.

Harcourt • Reading Skills Assessment

Reading Skill
Prescriptions for Reteaching

TOUCH A DREAM/THEME 1			
Skill	**Criterion Score**	**TE**	**PB**
Use prefixes and suffixes to decode	6/8	T118–119, T142, T173, T217, R4	17, 18, 24
Understand vocabulary meanings	9/12	T19, T52–53, T69, T100–101, T117, T146–147, T163, T188–189, T205, T230–231	1, 5, 8, 14, 23, 27, 30, 40
Understand narrative elements	6/8	T20–21, T50, T85, T133, R2	3, 4, 9
Understand characters' feelings and actions	3/4	T70–71, T98–99, T127, T215, R3	11, 15, 150

Harcourt • Reading Skills Assessment

Reading Skill
Prescriptions for Reteaching

TOUCH A DREAM/THEME 2			
Skill	**Criterion Score**	**TE**	**PB**
Understand vocabulary meanings	15/20	T271, T290, T307, T332–333, T349, T372–373, T389, T422–423, T439, T466–467	36, 43, 49, 59, 67
Predict outcomes	3/4	T272–273, T288–289, T319, T405, T409, R26	38, 39, 44, 61
Identify cause-effect relationships	3/4	T350–351, T368, T397, T453, R28	52, 53, 60

Harcourt • Reading Skills Assessment

Scoring/Interpreting

Reading Skill
Prescriptions for Reteaching

TOUCH A DREAM/THEME 3			
Skill	**Criterion Score**	**TE**	**PB**
Understand vocabulary meanings	9/12	T511, T534–535, T551, T580–581, T597, T624–625, T641, T672–673, T689, T716–717	75, 80, 83, 90, 97, 105, 106
Draw conclusions	3/4	T512–513, T532–533, T559, T655, R50	78, 79, 84
Recognize the sequence of events	3/4	T598–599, T622–623, T647, T701, R52	93, 94
Recognize comparisons and contrasts	3/4	T552–553, T578–579, T703, R51	86, 91

Scoring/Interpreting

Reading Skill
Prescriptions for Reteaching

TOUCH A DREAM/THEME 4			
Skill	**Criterion Score**	**TE**	**PB**
Understand vocabulary meanings	15/20	T751, T778–779, T795, T814–815, T831, T850–851, T867, T888–889, T905, T936–937	112, 119, 123, 126, 130, 133, 139, 142
Identify main idea and details	6/8	T752–753, T774–775, T801, T837, R74	114, 115, 120
Recognize a summary and a paraphrase	3/4	T832–833, T848–849, T879, T919, R77	128, 129, 134

Reading Skill
Prescriptions for Reteaching

TOUCH A DREAM/THEME 5			
Skill	**Criterion Score**	**TE**	**PB**
Understand vocabulary meanings	9/12	T979, T1004–1005, T1021, T1046, T1063, T1090–1091, T1107, T1132–1133, T1149, T1172–1173	145, 152, 155, 163, 171, 176, 179
Distinguish between fact and opinion	3/4	T980–981, T1000–1001, T1033, R98	148, 149, 157
Recognize author's purpose and perspective	3/4	T1064–1065, T1086–1087, T1115, T1155, R101	165, 166, 172
Locating information (book parts)	6/8	T1002–1003, T1027, R99	150, 151, 156

Reading Skill
Prescriptions for Reteaching

TOUCH A DREAM/THEME 6			
Skill	**Criterion Score**	**TE**	**PB**
Understand vocabulary meanings	12/16	T1207, T1240–1241, T1257, T1282–1283, T1299, T1324–1325, T1341, T1368–1369, T1385, T1412–1413	185, 191, 194, 200, 208, 214, 218
Use context clues	6/8	T1208–1209, T1238–1239, T1313, R122	189, 190, 201
Interpret graphic sources	6/8	T1300-1301, T1322–1323, T1355, R124	205, 205

Reduced and Annotated
Pupil Edition Facsimile Pages

∙∙

Touch a Dream/Theme 1

Name _____ Reading Skills Assessment

DECODING: Word Structure

Directions: Read each sentence. Fill in the answer circle in front of the word that best completes each sentence.

1. Some people will not get a place to sit if we _____ the number of chairs we need.
   - Ⓐ countable
   - Ⓑ miscount
   - Ⓒ recount
   - Ⓓ countless

2. I will _____ the bill today so that there will be no charges to pay later.
   - Ⓐ prepay
   - Ⓑ paying
   - Ⓒ underpay
   - Ⓓ payable

3. Did you _____ your yard with a fence?
   - Ⓐ foreclose
   - Ⓑ unclose
   - Ⓒ enclose
   - Ⓓ closed

4. I have trouble finding shoes that fit because my foot is _____ in size and shape.
   - Ⓐ irregular
   - Ⓑ regularity
   - Ⓒ regularly
   - Ⓓ regularize

GO ON →

Name _____ Reading Skills Assessment

DECODING: Word Structure (continued)

5. Gina made a low score on the test because most of her answers were _____ .
   - Ⓐ correctly
   - Ⓑ correctness
   - Ⓒ overcorrect
   - Ⓓ incorrect

6. Do not go near that snake because it is _____!
   - Ⓐ poisons
   - Ⓑ poisonous
   - Ⓒ poisonless
   - Ⓓ poisoned

7. He wears a crown as a symbol of his _____ .
   - Ⓐ royalty
   - Ⓑ royalize
   - Ⓒ royally
   - Ⓓ royalist

8. We will make an _____ later to tell who won the contest.
   - Ⓐ announces
   - Ⓑ announcement
   - Ⓒ unannounced
   - Ⓓ misannounce

STOP

Name _____ Reading Skills Assessment

VOCABULARY: Selection Vocabulary

Directions: Read each sentence. Fill in the answer circle in front of the word that best completes each sentence.

9. Todd has on a bright red shirt, so you will have no trouble _____ him.
   - Ⓐ listening
   - Ⓑ dining
   - Ⓒ recognizing
   - Ⓓ waving

10. We play ball each afternoon in the _____ lot near our school.
    - Ⓐ comfort
    - Ⓑ vacant
    - Ⓒ guided
    - Ⓓ fastened

11. The students have been _____ up the room to make it look nice.
    - Ⓐ sprucing
    - Ⓑ acting
    - Ⓒ longing
    - Ⓓ vanishing

12. Luke felt a bit _____ about starting such a difficult job.
    - Ⓐ uneasy
    - Ⓑ faulty
    - Ⓒ decorated
    - Ⓓ swift

GO ON →

Name _____ Reading Skills Assessment

VOCABULARY: Selection Vocabulary (continued)

13. Sticking with a task and showing _____ is a good way to succeed.
    - Ⓐ edges
    - Ⓑ perseverance
    - Ⓒ accidents
    - Ⓓ drifts

14. Tena enjoys reading during her _____ time.
    - Ⓐ leisure
    - Ⓑ skillful
    - Ⓒ collapsed
    - Ⓓ familiar

15. I hope we have several _____ to get ready for the talent show.
    - Ⓐ stale
    - Ⓑ damaged
    - Ⓒ rehearsals
    - Ⓓ dreadful

16. Our neighborhood has many _____ who teach us about customs in other countries.
    - Ⓐ immigrants
    - Ⓑ departments
    - Ⓒ bargains
    - Ⓓ fortunes

GO ON →

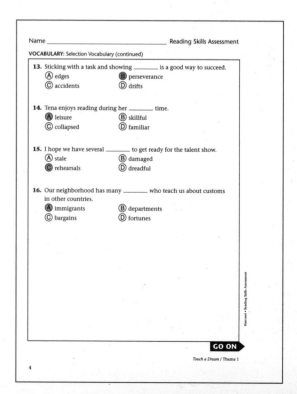

Touch a Dream/Theme 1

VOCABULARY: Selection Vocabulary (continued)

17. Her bravery in the face of danger inspired others to be _____, too.
- Ⓐ contented
- Ⓑ courageous
- Ⓒ chased
- Ⓓ angered

18. Because of his good _____, that athlete is highly respected.
- Ⓐ royalty
- Ⓑ failure
- Ⓒ subject
- Ⓓ sportsmanship

19. The student _____ searched the school for her missing project.
- Ⓐ timely
- Ⓑ tightly
- Ⓒ frantically
- Ⓓ coldly

20. He believed me because I looked him in the eye and spoke _____ .
- Ⓐ closely
- Ⓑ earnestly
- Ⓒ silently
- Ⓓ faintly

STOP

LITERARY CONCEPTS: Narrative Elements

Directions: Read each passage. Fill in the answer circle in front of the correct answer for each question.

Jimmy was feeling sad. When he got home from school, he called for his dog, Spike, to come play with him, just as he did every day after school. This time, though, Spike did not come.

"I think your dog may be gone," Mother said. "I saw him chasing a cat earlier today. I called for him to come back, but he kept on running after the cat. I haven't seen him since."

"What are we going to do?" Jimmy asked. "We've got to find him!"

"Don't worry," Mother said. "When it gets closer to supper time, I'm sure he'll find his way back home."

Jimmy went up to his room to do his homework, but he couldn't stop worrying about Spike. Later that evening, there was a scratching sound at the kitchen door. Jimmy ran to the door, opened it, and was relieved to see Spike there.

"Good boy! You're back! I missed you! Don't ever worry me like that again," Jimmy said.

GO ON

LITERARY CONCEPTS: Narrative Elements (continued)

21. The main character in this story is _____ .
- Ⓐ a cat
- Ⓑ Jimmy
- Ⓒ Mother
- Ⓓ Spike

22. When does the story take place?
- Ⓐ before breakfast
- Ⓑ during school
- Ⓒ after school
- Ⓓ during the night

23. What is the problem in the story?
- Ⓐ Mother will not let Jimmy have a dog.
- Ⓑ Jimmy's dog is missing.
- Ⓒ Jimmy's dog will not eat his food.
- Ⓓ A cat owner is angry that Spike chased the cat.

24. How is the problem in the story solved?
- Ⓐ Jimmy talks his mother into letting him get a new dog.
- Ⓑ Jimmy builds a dog pen so that Spike can't chase the cat again.
- Ⓒ Mother buys another kind of dog food for Jimmy's dog.
- Ⓓ Jimmy's dog comes home, safe and sound.

GO ON

LITERARY CONCEPTS: Narrative Elements (continued)

Barbara's family flew from Texas to Germany. They arrived on a cold, rainy day in September. Barbara's father had just been assigned to a military base near Frankfurt. The family was not getting off to a very good start. They arrived late, and no place on the base was open for supper. They took a taxi to a restaurant near the base, but the menu was in German. No one in the family had learned the language yet. They had to guess at what they ordered. When the waiter brought their food, Barbara ended up with liver soup! She ate a little of it, but she really didn't like liver at all.

"I'm not sure I'm going to like living here," Barbara said to her dad just before she went to bed that night. "Everything is so different! I don't see how I'm ever going to learn to speak German."

"It'll get better, Barb," her father reassured her. "You're going to love traveling to France, Italy, and other countries. And starting tomorrow, you, Mom, and I are signed up to take German lessons. Once you learn a few words and phrases, you'll feel more at ease here. I bet you have already learned the words for liver soup!"

"You're right, Dad," Barb laughed. "Looks like I may be a fast learner after all!"

GO ON

Annotated Facsimiles

Harcourt • Reading Skills Assessment

Touch a Dream/Theme 1

LITERARY CONCEPTS: Narrative Elements (continued)

25. The main character in this story is _____ .
- Ⓐ a restaurant waiter
- Ⓑ Dad
- Ⓒ Barbara
- Ⓓ Mom

26. Where does the story take place?
- Ⓐ Texas
- Ⓑ France
- Ⓒ Germany
- Ⓓ Italy

27. What is the problem in the story?
- Ⓐ Barbara does not want to fly to Germany.
- Ⓑ Barbara needs to learn a new language and adjust to a new country.
- Ⓒ Barbara's family cannot find housing near the military base.
- Ⓓ Barbara's father does not like his new job.

28. The events in the story take place over a period of _____.
- Ⓐ hours
- Ⓑ weeks
- Ⓒ months
- Ⓓ years

STOP

LITERARY CONCEPTS: Characters' Feelings and Actions

Directions: Read the passage. Fill in the answer circle in front of the correct answer for each question.

Patrick wanted to win the school spelling bee more than anything. He had been practicing for weeks, looking up words in the dictionary and spelling them out loud until he knew them by heart. He knew, though, that he had some stiff competition in the form of his best friend, Melissa Sanchez. Melissa seemed able to spell any word without even having to study.

Finally the day of the spelling bee came. As the contest went on, more and more students had to go back to their seats, having missed the words they were given. No one was surprised to see that the last two students in the contest were Patrick and Melissa.

Mrs. Connors called out the word that Melissa was to spell: *germane*. Melissa began to spell out loud: "G-e-r-m-a-i-n."

"I'm sorry, Melissa. That's incorrect," Mrs. Connors said. "Patrick, spell *germane*."

"G-e-r-m-a-n-e," Patrick said, with confidence. It was one of the words he had practiced.

"That's correct. Patrick, you're our new spelling champion."

Melissa went over to congratulate Patrick, who was smiling from ear to ear. "I'm happy for you, Patrick. It looks as if all your studying paid off. Maybe I should have practiced more instead of being so sure of myself."

GO ON

Touch a Dream/Theme 2

LITERARY CONCEPTS: Characters' Feelings and Actions (continued)

29. Which word can best be used to describe Patrick?
- Ⓐ cocky
- Ⓑ shy
- Ⓒ hardworking
- Ⓓ humorous

30. What does Patrick do to try to win the spelling bee?
- Ⓐ He tries to convince Melissa not to be in the contest.
- Ⓑ He asks Mrs. Connors to give him extra help after school.
- Ⓒ He asks Melissa to miss her word on purpose.
- Ⓓ He practices spelling words from a dictionary.

31. You can tell from Melissa's actions at the end of the story that she is _____ .
- Ⓐ a good sport
- Ⓑ jealous of Patrick
- Ⓒ angry about the word she missed
- Ⓓ uninterested in spelling

32. At the end of the story, Patrick most likely feels _____ .
- Ⓐ bored
- Ⓑ happy
- Ⓒ afraid
- Ⓓ nervous

STOP

VOCABULARY: Selection Vocabulary

Directions: Read each sentence. Fill in the answer circle in front of the word that best completes each sentence.

1. Frank was afraid he might get lost, since he was in an _____ area.
- Ⓐ amount
- Ⓑ obeyed
- Ⓒ unfamiliar
- Ⓓ attention

2. The scouts looked for a _____ in the thick brush so that they could make camp there.
- Ⓐ teller
- Ⓑ clearing
- Ⓒ combination
- Ⓓ program

3. After the storm, Bess _____ the clean air, enjoying the smell the rain had left behind.
- Ⓐ inhaled
- Ⓑ fastened
- Ⓒ warned
- Ⓓ arranged

4. The pale _____ flowers on that vine make the whole garden look beautiful.
- Ⓐ invisible
- Ⓑ lavender
- Ⓒ wailing
- Ⓓ satisfied

GO ON

Annotated Facsimiles

Harcourt • Reading Skills Assessment

Touch a Dream/Theme 2

VOCABULARY: Selection Vocabulary (continued)

5. At first the cubs stay near their mother, but soon they will _____ out on their own.
- Ⓐ clutch
- Ⓑ signal
- Ⓒ venture
- Ⓓ shun

6. The kitten climbed too high and was _____ at the top of the tree.
- Ⓐ cashed
- Ⓑ stranded
- Ⓒ repaired
- Ⓓ bid

7. Some birds _____ know to fly south for the winter.
- Ⓐ foolishly
- Ⓑ wishfully
- Ⓒ loosely
- Ⓓ instinctively

8. The glass vase is _____ and will break easily if you drop it.
- Ⓐ fragile
- Ⓑ confident
- Ⓒ serious
- Ⓓ patient

GO ON

VOCABULARY: Selection Vocabulary (continued)

9. The long drive was _____, so we went straight to bed when we got home.
- Ⓐ fresh
- Ⓑ exhausting
- Ⓒ supported
- Ⓓ feasting

10. Do not laugh when my brother acts silly or you might _____ him to act silly again.
- Ⓐ encourage
- Ⓑ earn
- Ⓒ catch
- Ⓓ range

11. I am sorry to say that I felt _____ when my friend got a new bike.
- Ⓐ rhymed
- Ⓑ coiled
- Ⓒ crowded
- Ⓓ jealous

12. As the _____ began telling the story, the actors made their way onto the stage.
- Ⓐ restaurant
- Ⓑ absence
- Ⓒ narrator
- Ⓓ puzzle

GO ON

VOCABULARY: Selection Vocabulary (continued)

13. I can tell from your _____ expression that you are happy today.
- Ⓐ tall
- Ⓑ loud
- Ⓒ grooved
- Ⓓ facial

14. Some animals are thought of as _____ because there are so few of them left.
- Ⓐ visited
- Ⓑ worked
- Ⓒ endangered
- Ⓓ covered

15. We looked forward to the class party with eager _____ .
- Ⓐ anticipation
- Ⓑ investigation
- Ⓒ worries
- Ⓓ chores

16. We saw no one around, so we decided that the island was _____ .
- Ⓐ uninhabited
- Ⓑ educated
- Ⓒ listened
- Ⓓ behaved

GO ON

VOCABULARY: Selection Vocabulary (continued)

17. On some days my hair won't do anything I like, but on other days it is more _____ .
- Ⓐ returnable
- Ⓑ manageable
- Ⓒ excitable
- Ⓓ drinkable

18. The dog showed his _____ by knocking over his water dish.
- Ⓐ rescue
- Ⓑ displeasure
- Ⓒ lesson
- Ⓓ survival

19. To play ball well you need to have good hand-eye _____ .
- Ⓐ disappointment
- Ⓑ questions
- Ⓒ coordination
- Ⓓ celebration

20. The plants were _____ into the country, even though they might carry harmful insects.
- Ⓐ rested
- Ⓑ smuggled
- Ⓒ reminded
- Ⓓ sounded

STOP

Annotated Facsimiles

Harcourt • Reading Skills Assessment

Touch a Dream/Theme 2

COMPREHENSION: Predict Outcomes

Directions: Read each passage. Fill in the answer circle in front of the correct answer for each question.

Jared and his dad were camping out near a lake. They were sleeping in sleeping bags inside a large tent. Very early one morning Jared got up, picked up a spade and a tin can, went outside the tent, and began to dig up worms to use as bait. When he had quite a few worms in the can, he grabbed his fishing pole.

"If we want to catch anything to cook for breakfast, we'd better get going, Jared," his dad said.

"I'm ready!" Jared answered. "I hope the fish are as hungry as I am!"

21. What are Jared and his dad most likely to do now?
    - (A) hike up a mountain
    - (B) fish in the nearby lake
    - (C) take down their tent
    - (D) get into their sleeping bags

22. What will Jared and Dad probably eat for breakfast?
    - (A) pancakes
    - (B) bacon
    - (C) fish
    - (D) cereal

GO ON

COMPREHENSION: Predict Outcomes (continued)

At school, Kerry's social studies class is studying about the pyramids in Egypt. The teacher gives each student a homework assignment. After school, Kerry goes to the public library, finds the section of the library that has sets of encyclopedia, and takes Volume *P* from the shelf. He opens the encyclopedia, reads for a while, and takes some notes on what he has read. Then he puts the book back on the shelf.

23. What will Kerry most likely do with the notes he took?
    - (A) throw them away
    - (B) give them to a friend
    - (C) use them to write a report
    - (D) use them to cover a textbook

24. What will Kerry probably do in social studies class tomorrow?
    - (A) give a talk on pyramids to his class
    - (B) ask where the public library is
    - (C) explain how to take notes
    - (D) ask his teacher for a different assignment

STOP

COMPREHENSION: Cause and Effect

Directions: Read each passage. Fill in the answer circle in front of the correct answer for each question.

Jess did an experiment to find out the effects of light on green plants. First, he got six small plants that looked the same in every way. Next, he put two of the plants near a sunny window, two in a dark closet, and two on a table in the hallway that did not get much light. He watered the plants as needed. At the end of three weeks, he checked the plants and found that the two plants that had been near the sunny window were much taller than before, and they looked healthy. The plants on the table were alive, but they looked pale and hadn't grown much. The two plants in the closet had died.

25. The plants in the closet probably died because they _____ .
    - (A) got too much water
    - (B) had bad soil
    - (C) did not get enough light
    - (D) were eaten by bugs

26. Why is Jess most likely to put plants near the window from now on?
    - (A) The soil in the plant pots needs to get fresh air.
    - (B) Plants need sunlight to grow and stay healthy.
    - (C) Plants put there will need less water.
    - (D) Flowers will look better near the window.

GO ON

COMPREHENSION: Cause and Effect (continued)

Sand is made up of loose grains of minerals or rocks. Most grains of sand are parts of solid rocks that have crumbled away. Rocks can become broken down in several ways. Some rocks crumble because they are affected by air, rain, or frost. Strong waves beating against rocks can also break them down.

Sand appears in many places on Earth. It can be found at the bottom of the sea, shallow lakes, or rivers. Great amounts of sand are found on beaches. In deserts, sand can cover hundreds of miles. It is often piled up by the wind in hills called sand *dunes*.

27. The passage says that rocks break down into sand because _____ .
    - (A) machines grind the rocks
    - (B) air, rain, frost, or waves affect the rocks
    - (C) fires turn the rocks into ash
    - (D) people crush the rocks by walking on them

28. Why do sand dunes form in the desert?
    - (A) Wind blows the sand into hills.
    - (B) Rain makes the sand stick together in clumps.
    - (C) Heat causes some parts to expand.
    - (D) Pressure underground forces the sand up.

STOP

Annotated Facsimiles

Harcourt • Reading Skills Assessment

Touch a Dream/Theme 3

VOCABULARY: Selection Vocabulary

Directions: Read each sentence. Fill in the answer circle in front of the word that best completes each sentence.

1. The shivering puppy seemed to be _____ by the loud thunder.
- Ⓐ hungered
- Ⓑ alarmed
- Ⓒ wanted
- Ⓓ tasted

2. We could hear the soft _____ of the leaves in the trees.
- Ⓐ rustle
- Ⓑ business
- Ⓒ practice
- Ⓓ respect

3. I would understand my lessons better if I had someone to _____ me.
- Ⓐ travel
- Ⓑ bloom
- Ⓒ tutor
- Ⓓ harvest

4. It upsets me to hear you and your sister _____ with each other.
- Ⓐ bicker
- Ⓑ collect
- Ⓒ arrange
- Ⓓ plant

GO ON

VOCABULARY: Selection Vocabulary (continued)

5. We tried to calm my aunt, who is a very _____ person.
- Ⓐ metal
- Ⓑ excitable
- Ⓒ chewable
- Ⓓ frozen

6. Our plan was approved because it is clear and _____ .
- Ⓐ thorny
- Ⓑ sickly
- Ⓒ logical
- Ⓓ backward

7. We hoped the other team would give up, or _____ .
- Ⓐ surrender
- Ⓑ create
- Ⓒ spend
- Ⓓ instruct

8. As soon as the rain _____ , we can go outside to play.
- Ⓐ expresses
- Ⓑ collapses
- Ⓒ reaches
- Ⓓ ceases

GO ON

VOCABULARY: Selection Vocabulary (continued)

9. We have an _____ supply of food, so we won't go hungry.
- Ⓐ answered
- Ⓑ abundant
- Ⓒ ill
- Ⓓ empty

10. When we spend time together, my baby brother and I are _____ .
- Ⓐ bonding
- Ⓑ melting
- Ⓒ drizzling
- Ⓓ stinging

11. The rain forest is a natural _____ for many plants and animals.
- Ⓐ harness
- Ⓑ habitat
- Ⓒ toll
- Ⓓ sport

12. Once a plant dies, it _____ very quickly.
- Ⓐ denies
- Ⓑ decomposes
- Ⓒ deserves
- Ⓓ dances

STOP

COMPREHENSION: Draw Conclusions

Directions: Read the passage. Fill in the answer circle in front of the correct answer for each question.

I found a raccoon last spring during a camping trip. I took it home and fed it warm milk through a straw. Now it weighs more than fifteen pounds, and it eats everything. Mr. Brown, our neighbor, has said, "Bob, if your raccoon gets in my garden one more time, I'll make a coonskin cap out of him!" Eating isn't the only problem. My sister was really upset when my raccoon hid her gold ring in its nest.

It is spring again, and my raccoon seems restless. We ride slowly up the river in my canoe. We hear the sound of another raccoon on the shore. My raccoon answers with a soft call. Suddenly, it dives into the water and swims toward the sound. I wait for a long, long time. Finally, I turn the canoe around and paddle slowly home.

GO ON

Touch a Dream/Theme 3

COMPREHENSION: Draw Conclusions (continued)

13. The raccoon that Bob found was probably from _____.
- Ⓐ the wild
- Ⓑ a pet shop
- Ⓒ the circus
- Ⓓ a zoo

14. What word would Mr. Brown and Bob's sister use to describe the raccoon?
- Ⓐ adorable
- Ⓑ playful
- Ⓒ silly
- Ⓓ bothersome

15. Bob's raccoon jumped out of the boat because it wanted to _____.
- Ⓐ drink some water
- Ⓑ swim to Bob's house
- Ⓒ join the other raccoon
- Ⓓ play a game with Bob

16. At the end of the story, Bob most likely felt _____.
- Ⓐ sad
- Ⓑ angry
- Ⓒ shy
- Ⓓ happy

STOP

COMPREHENSION: Sequence

Directions: Read the passage. Fill in the answer circle in front of the correct answer for each question.

It is easy to make blueberry muffins using a box mix. First, get together all the things you will need: an egg, water, muffin tins, baking spray, strainer, can opener, small mixing bowl, and a large spoon.

Second, preheat the oven to 400°.

Third, put baking spray into each muffin cup to keep the muffins from sticking.

Next, open the can of blueberries that comes in the mix. Pour the berries into a strainer and rinse them with water.

Then put one egg and 3/4 cup of water into the mixing bowl. Blend together with the spoon. Then add the muffin mix and stir until the egg, water, and mix are smooth.

After that, add the strained blueberries to the batter and mix them in with the spoon. Then spoon the batter into the greased muffin cups. Fill each cup about 3/4 full. Then bake about 20 minutes or until golden brown. Last, let the muffins cool about 5 minutes before serving them.

GO ON

COMPREHENSION: Sequence (continued)

17. What do you do **first** to make these blueberry muffins?
- Ⓐ Preheat the oven.
- Ⓑ Open the can of blueberries.
- Ⓒ Get together the things you will need.
- Ⓓ Put the egg and water into a bowl.

18. What do you do **right after** you mix in the blueberries?
- Ⓐ Blend the egg and water together with the spoon.
- Ⓑ Put baking spray into each muffin cup.
- Ⓒ Pour the berries into a strainer.
- Ⓓ Spoon the batter into the muffin cups.

19. What do you do **just before** baking the muffins?
- Ⓐ Put the egg and water into the mixing bowl.
- Ⓑ Fill each muffin cup about 3/4 full.
- Ⓒ Open the can of blueberries that comes in the mix.
- Ⓓ Put baking spray into each muffin cup.

20. What is the **last** step before serving the muffins?
- Ⓐ Let the muffins cool about 5 minutes.
- Ⓑ Stir the egg, water, and mix until smooth.
- Ⓒ Rinse the berries with water.
- Ⓓ Add the strained berries to the batter.

STOP

COMPREHENSION: Compare and Contrast

Directions: Read the passage. Fill in the answer circle in front of the correct answer for each question.

Lions and tigers are the largest animals in the cat family. Some people say the tiger is fiercer than the lion, but the lion is still thought to be among the strongest and fiercest of all wild creatures.

The bodies of tigers and lions are similar, but they can look quite different. A lion's coat can vary from buff yellow, orange-brown, or silver gray to dark brown. Male lions usually have a mane, which may be short or long and light or dark. Tigers are known for their striped markings. Depending on the type of tiger and the place where it lives, a tiger's coat may be bright reddish tan with dark stripes, or it may be paler or black and white. The tiger has no mane.

Both lions and tigers are meat eaters, and they usually hunt at night. They prefer to prey upon medium- to large-size animals such as zebras and antelopes, but they have been known to attack much larger animals.

Lions are unique among cats in that they live and hunt in a group, or *pride*. A pride is made up of several generations of lionesses (female lions), their cubs, and one or two adult male lions. Tigers usually live alone.

GO ON

Harcourt • Reading Skills Assessment

Page 9

Name _____ Reading Skills Assessment

COMPREHENSION: Compare and Contrast (continued)

21. According to this passage, both tigers and lions can be described as _____ .
- Ⓐ fierce
- Ⓑ quiet
- Ⓒ tame
- Ⓓ friendly

22. One way that tigers and lions are the same is that they both _____ .
- Ⓐ have bright reddish tan fur
- Ⓑ have manes
- Ⓒ are members of the cat family
- Ⓓ live in prides

23. The coat of a tiger is different from the coat of a lion because the tiger's coat has _____ .
- Ⓐ spots
- Ⓑ thicker fur
- Ⓒ longer fur
- Ⓓ striped markings

24. One way tigers are different from lions is that tigers usually _____ .
- Ⓐ hunt at night
- Ⓑ live alone
- Ⓒ eat meat
- Ⓓ attack antelopes

STOP

Touch a Dream / Theme 3   Score _____   9

Page 1

Name _____ Reading Skills Assessment

VOCABULARY: Selection Vocabulary

Directions: Read each sentence. Fill in the answer circle in front of the word that best completes each sentence.

1. Tom invented a _____ that helps people open jars easily.
- Ⓐ delay
- Ⓑ hurdle
- Ⓒ device
- Ⓓ castle

2. We might need to _____ our plan since we now have less money to spend.
- Ⓐ remain
- Ⓑ admire
- Ⓒ modify
- Ⓓ amuse

3. Eat this nice, _____ bowl of soup to give you energy.
- Ⓐ strengthening
- Ⓑ molding
- Ⓒ juggling
- Ⓓ asking

4. He is _____ with his money, always putting some aside for the future.
- Ⓐ faint
- Ⓑ rash
- Ⓒ thrifty
- Ⓓ confused

GO ON

Touch a Dream / Theme 4   1

Page 2

Name _____ Reading Skills Assessment

VOCABULARY: Selection Vocabulary (continued)

5. Because I was so hungry, Mother gave me a _____ piece of the pie.
- Ⓐ rude
- Ⓑ generous
- Ⓒ developed
- Ⓓ gentle

6. I have always been _____ by animals, and I love to be near them.
- Ⓐ remarked
- Ⓑ faulted
- Ⓒ fascinated
- Ⓓ galloped

7. I learned my lines for the play by reading the _____ over and over.
- Ⓐ chance
- Ⓑ substitute
- Ⓒ comfort
- Ⓓ script

8. You have done me a serious _____ by saying that I did something wrong.
- Ⓐ injustice
- Ⓑ instant
- Ⓒ sketch
- Ⓓ weave

GO ON

2   *Touch a Dream / Theme 4*

Page 3

Name _____ Reading Skills Assessment

VOCABULARY: Selection Vocabulary (continued)

9. My friend _____ the newspaper as soon as she finishes reading it.
- Ⓐ wanders
- Ⓑ discards
- Ⓒ disables
- Ⓓ rebuilds

10. We should probably stay home, under the _____ .
- Ⓐ circumstances
- Ⓑ contents
- Ⓒ structures
- Ⓓ sections

11. The king _____ that taxes should be paid throughout the land.
- Ⓐ wrapped
- Ⓑ decreed
- Ⓒ wrinkled
- Ⓓ stalked

12. In times of _____ , many people go hungry.
- Ⓐ posture
- Ⓑ direction
- Ⓒ famine
- Ⓓ detail

GO ON

Touch a Dream / Theme 4   3

Annotated Facsimiles

Touch a Dream/Theme 4

VOCABULARY: Selection Vocabulary (continued)

13. The student received top honors for both athletic ability and _____ .
   (A) companion   (B) relationship
   (C) scholarship   (D) return

14. "I guess you think you're smart," she _____ .
   (A) retorted   (B) accepted
   (C) tossed   (D) repacked

15. We fastened the two ends of the paper together to make a _____ headband.
   (A) lost   (B) furious
   (C) flooded   (D) circular

16. I knew _____ that I would like you.
   (A) straightaway   (B) questioningly
   (C) confusingly   (D) getaway

GO ON

VOCABULARY: Selection Vocabulary (continued)

17. Burt could not be guilty because he had an _____ for the time of the crime.
   (A) energy   (B) amount
   (C) alibi   (D) instrument

18. "Someone, please help me!" the woman cried out _____ .
   (A) desperately   (B) secretly
   (C) safely   (D) tamely

19. The king's subjects _____ him to lower their taxes.
   (A) gained   (B) implored
   (C) answered   (D) invented

20. We will eat here often if we find the food _____ .
   (A) accidental   (B) emotional
   (C) acceptable   (D) breakable

STOP

COMPREHENSION: Main Idea and Details

Directions: Read each passage. Fill in the answer circle in front of the correct answer for each question.

   Air pollution has become a problem in many parts of our country today. When harmful substances end up in the air and make it unhealthy for us to breathe, we say that the air has become *polluted*.

   Most air pollution results from human activities, but *pollutants* (substances that make the air unhealthy) can come from natural sources, too. A volcano, for example, can give off clouds of matter and gas that can harm living things. Dust storms and smoke from forest fires also pollute the air. Other natural pollutants include such things as pollen and bacteria.

   Much of the manmade pollution in our country comes from vehicles, such as cars, trucks, buses, and airplanes. Other sources of manmade pollution are factories, power plants, furnaces, and the burning of garbage and other wastes.

   Air pollution can be harmful to both humans and animals. It can lead to breathing difficulties and other health problems for both young and old.

GO ON

COMPREHENSION: Main Idea and Details (continued)

21. What is the main idea of this passage?
   (A) A volcano can give off clouds of matter and gas that can harm living things.
   (B) Air pollution has become a problem in many parts of our country today.
   (C) Other sources of manmade pollution are factories, power plants, furnaces, and the burning of garbage.
   (D) Other natural pollutants include such things as dust, pollen, and bacteria.

22. Which of these is a source of manmade pollution?
   (A) televisions
   (B) books
   (C) medicines
   (D) trucks

23. Which of these is a source of natural pollution?
   (A) whales
   (B) volcanoes
   (C) rocks
   (D) stars

24. According to the passage, air pollution can lead to _____ .
   (A) health problems
   (B) forest fires
   (C) dust storms
   (D) bacteria growth

GO ON

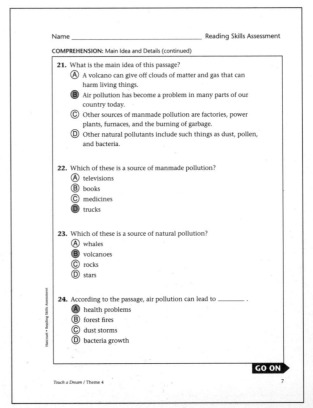

Annotated Facsimiles

Harcourt • Reading Skills Assessment

Touch a Dream/Theme 4

COMPREHENSION: Main Idea and Details (continued)

Railroads played an important part in helping the ranching industry in Texas to grow. In the early 1800s, there was not a lot of money to be made from raising cattle in Texas. Ranchers at that time raised cattle mostly for leather and for fat, which they used to make candles and soap. Later, people in cities in the East became eager to buy beef, and they were willing to pay a lot of money to get it. Ranchers could get ten times as much money for their cattle in the East as they could get in Texas. However, they had no good way to get the cattle from Texas to the cities in the East.

Railroads helped the ranchers by providing a way to get Texas cattle to distant markets. Ranchers began to organize cattle drives along trails that led from Texas through Oklahoma and north to "cow towns." The cow towns were places where *stockyards*, or cattle pens, were built near railroad lines. When the herds reached the stockyards, they could be loaded into railroad cars. The railroad cars could then carry the beef to markets in the East.

GO ON

COMPREHENSION: Main Idea and Details (continued)

25. What is this passage mostly about?
- (A) how to build and operate a railroad
- (B) how railroads helped Texas cattle ranchers
- (C) future plans for railroads in Texas
- (D) how to make candles and soap from beef fat

26. Ranchers wanted to sell their cattle in the East because _____ .
- (A) people in the East would pay more for beef
- (B) no one in Texas would buy beef
- (C) in Texas, beef could only be used to make leather
- (D) they wanted to help the railroads make money

27. Ranchers organized cattle drives to _____ .
- (A) move cattle to warmer places for the winter
- (B) bring new breeds of cattle from the East back to Texas
- (C) get their cattle to stockyards near railroads
- (D) keep cattle moving so they could not be stolen

28. Cow towns were important to ranchers because the cow towns _____ .
- (A) had cattle pens built near railroads
- (B) were all located in the East
- (C) had the best grazing land for cattle
- (D) were the best place to get supplies for cattle drives

STOP

COMPREHENSION: Summarize and Paraphrase

Directions: Read each passage. Fill in the answer circle in front of the correct answer for each question.

The Garza family had many things to do today. The weekend of the family picnic had finally arrived, and it was to be held in their backyard.

Carlos had to trim the bushes and mow the yard so that his younger brother, Joe, could arrange the tables and set up the folding chairs. Dad was cleaning the large barbecue grill and before long would start the fire. Mom had been cooking since dawn, with Delores and Frankie as her assistants. Will, the youngest, spent his time licking cake batter from the mixing bowls.

The morning was warm, and Joe's muscles ached. He wondered whether a family gathering was worth all this effort. Then he remembered that his grandmother always said that no matter what happens in life, you will always have your family to fall back on. He smiled at the memory and went back to work.

GO ON

COMPREHENSION: Summarize and Paraphrase (continued)

29. What is the best summary of this passage?
- (A) Joe remembered his grandmother saying that no matter what happens in life, you will always have your family to fall back on.
- (B) The men in the family did jobs like trimming bushes, mowing the yard, setting up tables, and cleaning the grill, while the women did the cooking.
- (C) The Garza family had many things to do to get ready for the family picnic, and Carlos, Joe, Dad, Mom, Delores, Frankie, and Will each had a job to do. Joe wondered if a family gathering was worth so much effort, but he decided it was.
- (D) The weekend of the family picnic had finally arrived. Everyone was excited about spending time together eating, telling stories, and playing games.

30. Which statement is the best paraphrase of this passage?
- (A) The Garzas had many things to do to prepare for an important family event.
- (B) Carlos had to trim the bushes and mow the lawn.
- (C) Mom had been cooking for days, aided by Delores, Frankie, and Will.
- (D) The morning was warm, and Joe's muscles ached.

GO ON

Annotated Facsimiles

[Page 12]

Name _____ Reading Skills Assessment

COMPREHENSION: Summarize and Paraphrase (continued)

Miranda's family was enjoying one last summer outing before school started—a day of hiking in the nearby mountains. As Miranda followed her family down the last leg of the trail, she slipped on a loose rock and fell with her left arm beneath her. She knew her wrist was hurt but didn't realize it was broken until her mother screamed. When they reached their car, they made a beeline for the closest hospital.

Before Miranda knew it, her arm was covered in an ugly cast. She was unhappy about starting fifth grade wearing a cast, but she decided to make the cast prettier by drawing colorful designs on it and by letting her family and friends write on it. "Now, that's better," Miranda thought.

31. Which of the following is the best summary of this passage?
   (A) While hiking with her family, Miranda slipped, broke her wrist, and had to wear a cast. She was unhappy about starting fifth grade in a cast until she decided to let her family and friends write on it.
   (B) Miranda's family had planned one last summer outing—a day of hiking in the nearby mountains.
   (C) Miranda hurt her wrist but did not know it was broken until her mother screamed.
   (D) Miranda was unhappy about starting fifth grade with a cast on her arm.

32. Which statement is the best paraphrase of this passage?
   (A) Miranda had become a little bored with summer vacation.
   (B) Miranda didn't realize her wrist was broken at first.
   (C) Miranda broke her wrist but made the best of wearing a cast.
   (D) Miranda and her family went hiking in the mountains.

STOP

12   Score _____   *Touch a Dream / Theme 4*

[Page 1]

Name _____ Reading Skills Assessment

VOCABULARY: Selection Vocabulary

Directions: Read each sentence. Fill in the answer circle in front of the word that best completes each sentence.

1. Those oil-soaked rags are highly _____ and should not be put near a fire.
   (A) flammable   (B) thinkable
   (C) rattled   (D) hiked

2. His _____ to the team is beyond question.
   (A) current   (B) dedication
   (C) body   (D) lantern

3. My friend _____ to me for breaking my pencil.
   (A) floated   (B) drifted
   (C) awaited   (D) apologized

4. We asked the students to help decorate the room, and they happily _____ .
   (A) wasted   (B) splashed
   (C) obliged   (D) tracked

GO ON

Touch a Dream / Theme 5   1

[Page 2]

Name _____ Reading Skills Assessment

VOCABULARY: Selection Vocabulary (continued)

5. We loved to dance along to the music my uncle played on the _____ .
   (A) privilege   (B) accordion
   (C) decoration   (D) costume

6. When she did not get her way, she would go _____ to her room to pout.
   (A) joyously   (B) smoothly
   (C) sulkily   (D) meltingly

7. A large lump _____ from his forehead where the ball had hit him.
   (A) protruded   (B) guarded
   (C) closed   (D) respected

8. I could tell by his medals that he was _____ a brave soldier.
   (A) undoubtedly   (B) swimmingly
   (C) hurriedly   (D) funnily

GO ON

2   *Touch a Dream / Theme 5*

[Page 3]

Name _____ Reading Skills Assessment

VOCABULARY: Selection Vocabulary (continued)

9. In class, we are studying the _____ of the ancient Egyptians.
   (A) breath   (B) fins
   (C) culture   (D) senses

10. At the party, we threw _____ and got it in our hair!
   (A) clouds   (B) confetti
   (C) mist   (D) mysteries

11. We play basketball every Friday night in the school _____ .
   (A) mountain   (B) certificate
   (C) document   (D) gymnasium

12. My parents set a _____ for my older brother so that he will come home at a certain time.
   (A) curfew   (B) photograph
   (C) dictionary   (D) relative

STOP

Touch a Dream / Theme 5   Score _____   3

Touch a Dream/Theme 5

COMPREHENSION: Fact and Opinion

Directions: Read the passage. Fill in the answer circle in front of the correct answer for each question.

Most people hate skunks. That is because skunks give off an unpleasant odor. Skunks are members of the weasel family. Weasels are unpopular animals, also. It is not surprising to learn that skunks and weasels are in the same family.

Skunks are strange-looking animals. They are about the size of a large house cat, and they have black and white markings. The white fur on a skunk's forehead and back look exactly as if someone painted a stripe right down its back. The skunk has an arched back, a broad forehead, and short legs. It moves rather slowly. A skunk looks silly when it walks.

A skunk has a pair of glands near its tail. When a skunk is frightened, these glands can give out a bad-smelling fluid to help defend it from its enemies. A skunk can shoot the fluid as far as ten feet into the air. The glands can be removed, and then skunks make the best pets in the world. Everyone should have a pet skunk at least once!

Skunks sleep during the day and come out at night. All farmers love skunks. This is because skunks eat insects, rats, mice, and other small animals that can hurt crops. Skunks also eat eggs, though, so they are not so helpful to farmers raising hens.

GO ON

COMPREHENSION: Fact and Opinion (continued)

13. Which of the following is a **fact** from the passage?
   Ⓐ Most people hate skunks.
   Ⓑ Weasels are unpopular animals.
   Ⓒ It is not surprising to learn that skunks and weasels are in the same family.
   ⬤ The skunk has an arched back, a broad forehead, and short legs.

14. Which of the following is an **opinion** from the passage?
   Ⓐ Skunks sleep during the day and come out at night.
   ⬤ Skunks make the best pets in the world.
   Ⓒ Skunks eat insects, rats, mice, and other small animals.
   Ⓓ Skunks also eat eggs.

15. Which of the following is a **fact** from the passage?
   Ⓐ Everyone should have a pet skunk at least once!
   Ⓑ A skunk looks silly when it walks.
   ⬤ Skunks are members of the weasel family.
   Ⓓ All farmers love skunks.

16. Which of the following is an **opinion** from the passage?
   Ⓐ Skunks have black and white markings.
   Ⓑ A skunk has a pair of glands near its tail.
   Ⓒ The glands can be removed.
   ⬤ Skunks are strange-looking animals.

STOP

COMPREHENSION: Author's Purpose and Perspective

Directions: Read each passage. Fill in the answer circle in front of the correct answer for each question.

Author 1

The Statue of Liberty is a large statue that stands in New York Harbor. France gave the statue to the United States in 1884 as a symbol of friendship and of the freedom that citizens enjoy under our form of government.

The statue shows a proud woman dressed in a loose robe. Her right arm holds a great torch raised high in the air. Her left arm holds a tablet bearing the date of the Declaration of Independence. On her head is a crown of spikes, like huge rays of the sun. At her feet is a broken shackle, which stands for the overthrowing of tyranny.

At the base of the statue is a poem, "The New Colossus," written by Emma Lazarus. The poem tells how the Statue of Liberty welcomes immigrants to America.

Author 2

There are many wonderful sights to see in New York, but there is only one sight that you really must see—the Statue of Liberty. It is one of the most beautiful sights in the world. So many times I have heard my grandmother tell about the first time she saw the statue when she and her family came to the United States to live. She said she knew that it meant they were welcome in America—land of the free.

The statue has welcomed many, many immigrants to our country. To people who may have left their homelands because of war, hunger, or fear, the statue is a symbol of hope, freedom, and a new chance at a good life. This is why you really must go to see the Statue of Liberty.

GO ON

COMPREHENSION: Author's Purpose and Perspective (continued)

17. The main purpose of Author 1 is to _____ .
   Ⓐ persuade   ⬤ inform
   Ⓒ entertain   Ⓓ warn

18. Which of the following statements would most likely be used by Author 1?
   Ⓐ The Statue of Liberty is the most beautiful sight in the entire world.
   ⬤ The Statue of Liberty stands 151 feet high and weighs about 450,000 pounds.
   Ⓒ No other sight in America could ever mean as much to visitors as the Statue of Liberty.
   Ⓓ The Statue of Liberty rises tall and proud and must never be removed because it is a symbol of hope for so many.

19. The main purpose of Author 2 is to _____ .
   ⬤ persuade   Ⓑ inform
   Ⓒ entertain   Ⓓ warn

20. Which of the following statements would most likely be used by Author 2?
   ⬤ The Statue of Liberty stands for all the hopes and dreams of people who first come to America.
   Ⓑ The Statue of Liberty serves no purpose but looks pretty.
   Ⓒ The Statue of Liberty should be moved out of New York Harbor.
   Ⓓ The Statue of Liberty costs too much to maintain and should be taken down.

STOP

STUDY AND RESEARCH SKILLS: Locating Information

Directions: Fill in the answer circle in front of the correct answer for each question.

21. Where should you look to find out when a book was published?
    - Ⓐ the table of contents
    - Ⓑ the copyright page
    - Ⓒ the index
    - Ⓓ the glossary

22. Where should you look to find biographical information about the author of a book?
    - Ⓐ the book jacket
    - Ⓑ the title page
    - Ⓒ the copyright page
    - Ⓓ the table of contents

23. Becky wants to know whether her social studies textbook has any information on the Great Plains. Where should she look to see whether this topic is in the book?
    - Ⓐ the cover
    - Ⓑ the title page
    - Ⓒ the index
    - Ⓓ the glossary

24. Hector does not know the meaning of a specialized term in his science book. Where should he look to find out the meaning of the word?
    - Ⓐ the book jacket
    - Ⓑ the table of contents
    - Ⓒ the index
    - Ⓓ the glossary

GO ON ▶

STUDY AND RESEARCH SKILLS: Locating Information (continued)

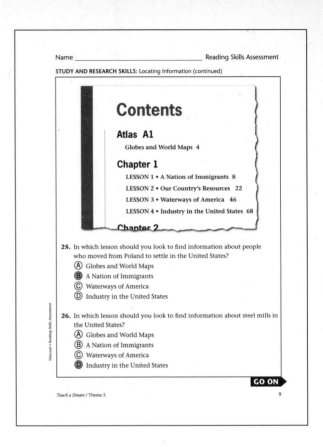

25. In which lesson should you look to find information about people who moved from Poland to settle in the United States?
    - Ⓐ Globes and World Maps
    - Ⓑ A Nation of Immigrants
    - Ⓒ Waterways of America
    - Ⓓ Industry in the United States

26. In which lesson should you look to find information about steel mills in the United States?
    - Ⓐ Globes and World Maps
    - Ⓑ A Nation of Immigrants
    - Ⓒ Waterways of America
    - Ⓓ Industry in the United States

GO ON ▶

Touch a Dream/Theme 6

STUDY AND RESEARCH SKILLS: Locating Information (continued)

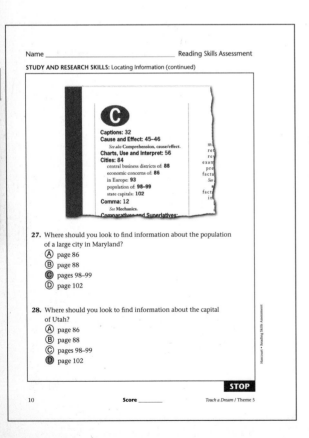

27. Where should you look to find information about the population of a large city in Maryland?
    - Ⓐ page 86
    - Ⓑ page 88
    - Ⓒ pages 98–99
    - Ⓓ page 102

28. Where should you look to find information about the capital of Utah?
    - Ⓐ page 86
    - Ⓑ page 88
    - Ⓒ pages 98–99
    - Ⓓ page 102

STOP ■

VOCABULARY: Selection Vocabulary

Directions: Read each sentence. Fill in the answer circle in front of the word that best completes each sentence.

1. You can be anything you want to be; the _____ are endless.
    - Ⓐ excuses
    - Ⓑ patients
    - Ⓒ possibilities
    - Ⓓ celebrations

2. The soldier ate his _____ of food for the day.
    - Ⓐ altitude
    - Ⓑ ration
    - Ⓒ network
    - Ⓓ years

3. The inventor had all kinds of interesting _____ in his workshop.
    - Ⓐ rescues
    - Ⓑ phases
    - Ⓒ winds
    - Ⓓ gadgets

4. We need an _____ to help us understand the foreign language.
    - Ⓐ alarm
    - Ⓑ existence
    - Ⓒ amateur
    - Ⓓ interpreter

GO ON ▶

Name _____ Reading Skills Assessment

VOCABULARY: Selection Vocabulary (continued)

5. The fans were screaming _____ at the end of the game.
   - (A) silently
   - (B) quietly
   - (C) hysterically
   - (D) gracefully

6. Those little sandwiches on the tray look _____ .
   - (A) whispered
   - (B) appetizing
   - (C) hopeful
   - (D) serious

7. As we walked, I _____ reached down to pet my dog.
   - (A) invisibly
   - (B) noisily
   - (C) occasionally
   - (D) dizzily

8. The butterwort eats insects, so it is a _____ plant.
   - (A) youthful
   - (B) nervous
   - (C) sincere
   - (D) carnivorous

Name _____ Reading Skills Assessment

VOCABULARY: Selection Vocabulary (continued)

9. My cake tasted bad because I _____ mixed in salt instead of sugar.
   - (A) highly
   - (B) accidentally
   - (C) wholly
   - (D) weakly

10. The spider will catch a _____ in its web.
    - (A) victim
    - (B) hike
    - (C) plaster
    - (D) legend

11. We _____ our cafeteria into a beautiful garden by using flowers and foil to decorate.
    - (A) trickled
    - (B) transformed
    - (C) puzzled
    - (D) breathed

12. Mr. Clark will _____ to solve the mystery for us.
    - (A) investigate
    - (B) empty
    - (C) ooze
    - (D) fasten

Name _____ Reading Skills Assessment

VOCABULARY: Selection Vocabulary (continued)

13. That is the mother wolf, and these are her pups, _____ .
    - (A) lowly
    - (B) apparently
    - (C) daintily
    - (D) carefully

14. We tried not to make noise as we tiptoed along the long _____ .
    - (A) friction
    - (B) century
    - (C) sample
    - (D) corridor

15. An early _____ in America most likely had to grow his vegetables and hunt for his meat.
    - (A) pioneer
    - (B) monument
    - (C) statue
    - (D) fabric

16. The two sisters sing in perfect _____ .
    - (A) harmony
    - (B) carelessness
    - (C) capitals
    - (D) denials

Name _____ Reading Skills Assessment

VOCABULARY: Vocabulary in Context

Directions: Read each passage. Fill in the answer circle in front of the correct answer for each question.

The score in our baseball game was tied. On the last play of the game, I was playing outfield when a fly ball came toward me. I really tried to catch it, but I dropped the ball. The umpire called it an <u>error</u>, and the other team scored. Later, in the players' locker room, I could hear the <u>tread</u> of sneakers coming toward me. I recognized our coach's familiar walk. What would he say to me about causing us to lose the game?

17. The word <u>error</u> in this passage means _____ .
    - (A) wrong measure
    - (B) misplay in baseball
    - (C) mistake or accident
    - (D) false belief

18. The word <u>tread</u> in this passage means _____ .
    - (A) hurt someone's feelings
    - (B) grooves on a tire
    - (C) step or walk
    - (D) staying upright in water

Harcourt • Reading Skills Assessment

Annotated Facsimiles

Touch a Dream/Theme 6

Mel <u>resembled</u> his twin brother Seth so much that they looked almost exactly the same.

"It is just <u>incredible</u> how much you two boys look alike," their neighbor said. "I mean, it is just hard to believe that two people could look so much alike in every way."

19. The word <u>resembled</u> in this passage means _____ .
- (A) tricked
- (B) disliked
- (C) amused
- **(D) looked like**

20. The word <u>incredible</u> in this passage means _____ .
- **(A) unbelievable**
- (B) annoying
- (C) tempting
- (D) honorable

Feeling butterflies in her stomach, Janice laid her notes on the <u>podium</u> and put her hands on the sides of the wooden stand so the audience couldn't see her hands or papers shaking. She knew if she forgot the poem she was to recite to the class, she would be <u>ridiculed</u> and laughed at for days. She did her best to breathe deeply and think only about the poem—not how many people were listening.

21. The word <u>podium</u> in this passage means _____ .
- (A) low wall
- **(B) stand for a speaker**
- (C) foot-shaped object
- (D) script

22. The word <u>ridiculed</u> in this passage means _____ .
- (A) angry
- (B) rhymed words
- **(C) made fun of**
- (D) breathed fast

Tony was totally <u>engrossed</u> in his book. The story was so interesting and his attention was so focused on what he was reading that he didn't even hear the bell ring. An <u>exodus</u> of students out of the classroom began, but Tony stayed in his seat, reading. Finally, his teacher said, "Tony, I'm so happy you're enjoying your book, but don't you think you should get to your next class?"

23. The word <u>engrossed</u> in this passage means _____ .
- (A) copied by hand
- **(B) interested or engaged**
- (C) bought in large amounts
- (D) stuck to

24. The word <u>exodus</u> in this passage means _____ .
- (A) loud noise
- **(B) mass exit**
- (C) sitting position
- (D) strong liking

Directions: Look at the graph and the chart that follow. Then read the questions that follow the graph or chart. Fill in the answer circle in front of the correct answer for each question.

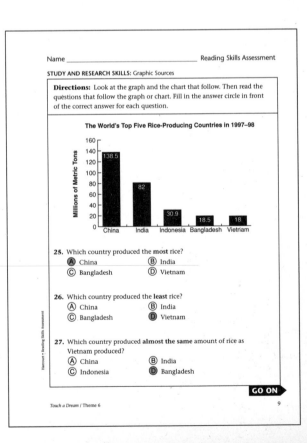

The World's Top Five Rice-Producing Countries in 1997–98

(bar graph, Millions of Metric Tons)
- China: 138.5
- India: 82
- Indonesia: 30.9
- Bangladesh: 18.5
- Vietnam: 18

25. Which country produced the **most** rice?
- **(A) China**
- (B) India
- (C) Bangladesh
- (D) Vietnam

26. Which country produced the **least** rice?
- (A) China
- (B) India
- (C) Bangladesh
- **(D) Vietnam**

27. Which country produced **almost the same** amount of rice as Vietnam produced?
- (A) China
- (B) India
- (C) Indonesia
- **(D) Bangladesh**

Harcourt • Reading Skills Assessment

Touch a Dream/Theme 6

Population History of Ten United States Cities from 1850–1900 (in thousands)						
	1850	1860	1870	1880	1890	1900
Atlanta	3	10	22	37	66	90
Boston	137	178	251	363	448	560
Chicago	30	109	299	503	1,100	1,698
Detroit	21	46	80	116	206	286
Houston	3	5	9	17	26	45
Los Angeles	2	4	6	11	50	102
Memphis	9	3	10	34	64	103
New York	696	1,175	1,478	1,912	2,507	3,437
Philadelphia	121	566	674	847	1,049	1,293
San Francisco	35	57	149	234	299	343

28. Which city had the **lowest** population **in 1880**?
   Ⓐ Los Angeles
   Ⓑ New York
   Ⓒ Philadelphia
   Ⓓ San Francisco

29. Which city had the **greatest** population **in 1880**?
   Ⓐ Los Angeles
   ● New York
   Ⓒ Philadelphia
   Ⓓ San Francisco

---

30. Which two cities had **almost the same** population **in 1900**?
   ● Los Angeles and Mempis
   Ⓑ Boston and Chicago
   Ⓒ Atlanta and Detroit
   Ⓓ Philadelphia and San Francisco

31. Which city's population **doubled between 1850 and 1860**?
   Ⓐ Atlanta
   Ⓑ Houston
   ● Los Angeles
   Ⓓ Memphis

32. Which city's population **got smaller between 1850 and 1860**?
   Ⓐ Atlanta
   Ⓑ Chicago
   Ⓒ Detroit
   ● Memphis

Annotated Facsimiles

Answer Key:
Reading Skills Assessment

Theme 1

DECODING:
Word Structure
Prefixes and Suffixes
1. B
2. A
3. C
4. A
5. D
6. B
7. A
8. B

VOCABULARY:
Selection Vocabulary
9. C
10. B
11. A
12. A
13. B
14. A
15. C
16. A
17. B
18. D
19. C
20. B

LITERARY CONCEPTS:
Narrative Elements
21. B
22. C
23. B
24. D
25. C
26. C
27. B
28. A

LITERARY CONCEPTS:
Characters' Feelings and Actions
29. C
30. D
31. A
32. B

Theme 2

VOCABULARY:
Selection Vocabulary
1. C
2. B
3. A
4. B
5. C
6. B
7. D
8. A
9. B
10. A
11. D
12. C
13. D
14. C
15. A
16. A
17. B
18. B
19. C
20. B

COMPREHENSION:
Predict Outcomes
21. B
22. C
23. C
24. A

COMPREHENSION:
Cause and Effect
25. C
26. B
27. B
28. A

Theme 3

VOCABULARY:
Selection Vocabulary
1. B
2. A
3. C
4. A
5. B
6. C
7. A
8. D
9. B
10. A
11. B
12. B

COMPREHENSION:
Draw Conclusions
13. A
14. D
15. C
16. A

COMPREHENSION:
Sequence
17. C
18. D
19. B
20. A

COMPREHENSION:
Compare and Contrast
21. A
22. C
23. D
24. B

Answer Key:
Reading Skills Assessment

Theme 4

VOCABULARY:
Selection Vocabulary
1. C
2. C
3. A
4. C
5. B
6. C
7. D
8. A
9. B
10. A
11. B
12. C
13. C
14. A
15. D
16. A
17. C
18. A
19. B
20. C

COMPREHENSION:
Main Idea and Details
21. B
22. D
23. B
24. A
25. B
26. A
27. C
28. A

COMPREHENSION:
Summarize and Paraphrase
29. C
30. A
31. A
32. C

Theme 5

VOCABULARY:
Selection Vocabulary
1. A
2. B
3. D
4. C
5. B
6. C
7. A
8. A
9. C
10. B
11. D
12. A

COMPREHENSION:
Fact and Opinion
13. D
14. B
15. C
16. D

COMPREHENSION:
Author's Purpose and Perspective
17. B
18. B
19. A
20. A

STUDY AND RESEARCH SKILLS: Locating Information
21. B
22. A
23. C
24. D
25. B
26. D
27. C
28. D

Theme 6

VOCABULARY:
Selection Vocabulary
1. C
2. B
3. D
4. D
5. C
6. B
7. C
8. D
9. B
10. A
11. B
12. A
13. B
14. D
15. A
16. A

VOCABULARY: Vocabulary in Context
17. B
18. C
19. D
20. A
21. B
22. C
23. B
24. B

STUDY AND RESEARCH SKILLS: Graphic Sources
25. A
26. D
27. D
28. A
29. B
30. A
31. C
32. D

Appendix

• •

Harcourt • Reading Skills Assessment

Student Record Form
Reading Skills Assessment

Collections Grade 4

Name _____ Grade _____

Teacher _____

Touch a Dream/Theme 1

	Number Possible	Criterion Score	Number Correct	Diagnostic Category
Use prefixes and suffixes to decode	8	6		
Understand vocabulary meanings	12	9		
Understand narrative elements	8	6		
Understand characters' feelings and actions	4	3		

Touch a Dream/Theme 2

	Number Possible	Criterion Score	Number Correct	Diagnostic Category
Understand vocabulary meanings	20	15		
Predict outcomes	4	3		
Identify cause-effect relationships	4	3		

Touch a Dream/Theme 3

	Number Possible	Criterion Score	Number Correct	Diagnostic Category
Understand vocabulary meanings	12	9		
Draw conclusions	4	3		
Recognize the sequence of events	4	3		
Recognize comparisons and contrasts	4	3		

Harcourt • Reading Skills Assessment

Student Record Form
Reading Skills Assessment

• •

Collections **Grade 4**

Name _____ Grade _____

Teacher _____

Touch a Dream/Theme 4

	Number Possible	Criterion Score	Number Correct	Diagnostic Category
Understand vocabulary meanings	20	15		
Identify main idea and details	8	6		
Recognize a summary and a paraphrase	4	3		

Touch a Dream/Theme 5

	Number Possible	Criterion Score	Number Correct	Diagnostic Category
Understand vocabulary meanings	12	9		
Distinguish between fact and opinion	4	3		
Recognize author's purpose and perspective	4	3		
Locating information (book parts)	8	6		

Touch a Dream/Theme 6

	Number Possible	Criterion Score	Number Correct	Diagnostic Category
Understand vocabulary meanings	16	12		
Use context clues	8	6		
Interpret graphic sources	8	6		

COLLECTIONS

Reading Skills Assessment

Touch a Dream / Theme 1

Name _____ Date _____

SKILL AREA	Criterion Score	Pupil Score	Pupil Strength
DECODING Word Structure Prefixes, Suffixes	6/8	_____	_____
VOCABULARY Selection Vocabulary	9/12	_____	_____
LITERARY CONCEPTS Narrative Elements (Characters, Setting, Plot)	6/8	_____	_____
Characters' Feelings and Actions	3/4	_____	_____
TOTAL SCORE	24/32	_____	_____

Were accommodations made in administering this test? ❑ Yes ❑ No

Type of accommodations: _____

_____

Printed in the United States of America

ISBN 0-15-314464-5

1 2 3 4 5 6 7 8 9 10 170 2003 2002 2001 2000

DECODING: Word Structure

> **Directions:** Read each sentence. Fill in the answer circle in front of the word that best completes each sentence.

1. Some people will not get a place to sit if we _____ the number of chairs we need.
   - Ⓐ countable
   - Ⓑ miscount
   - Ⓒ recount
   - Ⓓ countless

2. I will _____ the bill today so that there will be no charges to pay later.
   - Ⓐ prepay
   - Ⓑ paying
   - Ⓒ underpay
   - Ⓓ payable

3. Did you _____ your yard with a fence?
   - Ⓐ foreclose
   - Ⓑ unclose
   - Ⓒ enclose
   - Ⓓ closed

4. I have trouble finding shoes that fit because my foot is _____ in size and shape.
   - Ⓐ irregular
   - Ⓑ regularity
   - Ⓒ regularly
   - Ⓓ regularize

GO ON

DECODING: Word Structure (continued)

5. Gina made a low score on the test because most of her answers
were _____ .

Ⓐ correctly   Ⓑ correctness

Ⓒ overcorrect   Ⓓ incorrect

6. Do not go near that snake because it is _____!

Ⓐ poisons   Ⓑ poisonous

Ⓒ poisonless   Ⓓ poisoned

7. He wears a crown as a symbol of his _____ .

Ⓐ royalty   Ⓑ royalize

Ⓒ royally   Ⓓ royalist

8. We will make an _____ later to tell who won the contest.

Ⓐ announces   Ⓑ announcement

Ⓒ unannounced   Ⓓ misannounce

STOP

Score _____

VOCABULARY: Selection Vocabulary

Directions: Read each sentence. Fill in the answer circle in front of the word that best completes each sentence.

9. Todd has on a bright red shirt, so you will have no trouble _____ him.
Ⓐ listening   Ⓑ dining
Ⓒ recognizing   Ⓓ waving

10. We play ball each afternoon in the _____ lot near our school.
Ⓐ comfort   Ⓑ vacant
Ⓒ guided   Ⓓ fastened

11. The students have been _____ up the room to make it look nice.
Ⓐ sprucing   Ⓑ acting
Ⓒ longing   Ⓓ vanishing

12. Luke felt a bit _____ about starting such a difficult job.
Ⓐ uneasy   Ⓑ faulty
Ⓒ decorated   Ⓓ swift

GO ON

VOCABULARY: Selection Vocabulary (continued)

13. Sticking with a task and showing _____ is a good way to succeed.

Ⓐ edges   Ⓑ perseverance

Ⓒ accidents   Ⓓ drifts

14. Tena enjoys reading during her _____ time.

Ⓐ leisure   Ⓑ skillful

Ⓒ collapsed   Ⓓ familiar

15. I hope we have several _____ to get ready for the talent show.

Ⓐ harvests   Ⓑ damages

Ⓒ rehearsals   Ⓓ waters

16. Our neighborhood has many _____ who teach us about customs in other countries.

Ⓐ immigrants   Ⓑ departments

Ⓒ bargains   Ⓓ fortunes

GO ON

VOCABULARY: Selection Vocabulary (continued)

17. Her bravery in the face of danger inspired others to be _____, too.

   Ⓐ contented   Ⓑ courageous

   Ⓒ chased   Ⓓ angered

18. Because of his good _____, that athlete is highly respected.

   Ⓐ royalty   Ⓑ failure

   Ⓒ subject   Ⓓ sportsmanship

19. The student _____ searched the school for her missing project.

   Ⓐ timely   Ⓑ tightly

   Ⓒ frantically   Ⓓ coldly

20. He believed me because I looked him in the eye and spoke _____ .

   Ⓐ closely   Ⓑ earnestly

   Ⓒ silently   Ⓓ faintly

STOP

LITERARY CONCEPTS: Narrative Elements

Directions: Read each passage. Fill in the answer circle in front of the correct answer for each question.

Jimmy was feeling sad. When he got home from school, he called for his dog, Spike, to come play with him, just as he did every day after school. This time, though, Spike did not come.

"I think your dog may be gone," Mother said. "I saw him chasing a cat earlier today. I called for him to come back, but he kept on running after the cat. I haven't seen him since."

"What are we going to do?" Jimmy asked. "We've got to find him!"

"Don't worry," Mother said. "When it gets closer to supper time, I'm sure he'll find his way back home."

Jimmy went up to his room to do his homework, but he couldn't stop worrying about Spike. Later that evening, there was a scratching sound at the kitchen door. Jimmy ran to the door, opened it, and was relieved to see Spike there.

"Good boy! You're back! I missed you! Don't ever worry me like that again," Jimmy said.

GO ON

LITERARY CONCEPTS: Narrative Elements (continued)

21. The main character in this story is _____ .

Ⓐ a cat

Ⓑ Jimmy

Ⓒ Mother

Ⓓ Spike

22. When does the story take place?

Ⓐ before breakfast

Ⓑ during school

Ⓒ after school

Ⓓ during the night

23. What is the problem in the story?

Ⓐ Mother will not let Jimmy have a dog.

Ⓑ Jimmy's dog is missing.

Ⓒ Jimmy's dog will not eat his food.

Ⓓ A cat owner is angry that Spike chased the cat.

24. How is the problem in the story solved?

Ⓐ Jimmy talks his mother into letting him get a new dog.

Ⓑ Jimmy builds a dog pen so that Spike can't chase the cat again.

Ⓒ Mother buys another kind of dog food for Jimmy's dog.

Ⓓ Jimmy's dog comes home, safe and sound.

GO ON

LITERARY CONCEPTS: Narrative Elements (continued)

Barbara's family flew from Texas to Germany. They arrived on a cold, rainy day in September. Barbara's father had just been assigned to a military base near Frankfurt. The family was not getting off to a very good start. They arrived late, and no place on the base was open for supper. They took a taxi to a restaurant near the base, but the menu was in German. No one in the family had learned the language yet. They had to guess at what they ordered. When the waiter brought their food, Barbara ended up with liver soup! She ate a little of it, but she really didn't like liver at all.

"I'm not sure I'm going to like living here," Barbara said to her dad just before she went to bed that night. "Everything is so different! I don't see how I'm ever going to learn to speak German."

"It'll get better, Barb," her father reassured her. "You're going to love traveling to France, Italy, and other countries. And starting tomorrow, you, Mom, and I are signed up to take German lessons. Once you learn a few words and phrases, you'll feel more at ease here. I bet you have already learned the words for liver soup!"

"You're right, Dad," Barb laughed. "Looks like I may be a fast learner after all!"

LITERARY CONCEPTS: Narrative Elements (continued)

25. The main character in this story is _____ .

  (A) a restaurant waiter

  (B) Dad

  (C) Barbara

  (D) Mom

26. Where does the story take place?

  (A) Texas

  (B) France

  (C) Germany

  (D) Italy

27. What is the problem in the story?

  (A) Barbara does not want to fly to Germany.

  (B) Barbara needs to learn a new language and adjust to a new country.

  (C) Barbara's family cannot find housing near the military base.

  (D) Barbara's father does not like his new job.

28. The events in the story take place over a period of _____.

  (A) hours

  (B) weeks

  (C) months

  (D) years

STOP

LITERARY CONCEPTS: Characters' Feelings and Actions

Directions: Read the passage. Fill in the answer circle in front of the correct answer for each question.

Patrick wanted to win the school spelling bee more than anything. He had been practicing for weeks, looking up words in the dictionary and spelling them out loud until he knew them by heart. He knew, though, that he had some stiff competition in the form of his best friend, Melissa Sanchez. Melissa seemed able to spell any word without even having to study.

Finally the day of the spelling bee came. As the contest went on, more and more students had to go back to their seats, having missed the words they were given. No one was surprised to see that the last two students in the contest were Patrick and Melissa.

Mrs. Connors called out the word that Melissa was to spell: *germane*. Melissa began to spell out loud: "*G-e-r-m-a-i-n*."

"I'm sorry, Melissa. That's incorrect," Mrs. Connors said. "Patrick, spell *germane*."

"*G-e-r-m-a-n-e*," Patrick said, with confidence. It was one of the words he had practiced.

"That's correct. Patrick, you're our new spelling champion."

Melissa went over to congratulate Patrick, who was smiling from ear to ear. "I'm happy for you, Patrick. It looks as if all your studying paid off. Maybe I should have practiced more instead of being so sure of myself."

GO ON

LITERARY CONCEPTS: Characters' Feelings and Actions (continued)

29. Which word can best be used to describe Patrick?

Ⓐ cocky

Ⓑ shy

Ⓒ hardworking

Ⓓ humorous

30. What does Patrick do to try to win the spelling bee?

Ⓐ He tries to convince Melissa not to be in the contest.

Ⓑ He asks Mrs. Connors to give him extra help after school.

Ⓒ He asks Melissa to miss her word on purpose.

Ⓓ He practices spelling words from a dictionary.

31. You can tell from Melissa's actions at the end of the story that she is _____ .

Ⓐ a good sport

Ⓑ jealous of Patrick

Ⓒ angry about the word she missed

Ⓓ uninterested in spelling

32. At the end of the story, Patrick most likely feels _____ .

Ⓐ bored

Ⓑ happy

Ⓒ afraid

Ⓓ nervous

STOP

Harcourt • Reading Skills Assessment

You Can Do It! / Theme 1
Reading Skills Assessment

Orlando   Boston   Dallas   Chicago   San Diego

Part No. 9997-06741-X

ISBN 0-15-314464-5 (Package of 12)

4

COLLECTIONS

Reading Skills Assessment

Touch a Dream / Theme 2

Name _____ Date _____

SKILL AREA	Criterion Score	Pupil Score	Pupil Strength
VOCABULARY Selection Vocabulary	15/20	_____	_____
COMPREHENSION Predict Outcomes	3/4	_____	_____
Cause and Effect	3/4	_____	_____
TOTAL SCORE	21/28	_____	_____

Were accommodations made in administering this test? ☐ Yes ☐ No

Type of accommodations: _____

_____

ISBN 0-15-314464-5

1 2 3 4 5 6 7 8 9 10 170 2003 2002 2001 2000

VOCABULARY: Selection Vocabulary

Directions: Read each sentence. Fill in the answer circle in front of the word that best completes each sentence.

1. Frank was afraid he might get lost, since he was in an _____ area.
   - Ⓐ amount
   - Ⓑ obeyed
   - Ⓒ unfamiliar
   - Ⓓ attention

2. The scouts looked for a _____ in the thick brush so that they could make camp there.
   - Ⓐ teller
   - Ⓑ clearing
   - Ⓒ combination
   - Ⓓ program

3. After the storm, Bess _____ the clean air, enjoying the smell the rain had left behind.
   - Ⓐ inhaled
   - Ⓑ fastened
   - Ⓒ warned
   - Ⓓ arranged

4. The pale _____ flowers on that vine make the whole garden look beautiful.
   - Ⓐ invisible
   - Ⓑ lavender
   - Ⓒ wailing
   - Ⓓ satisfied

GO ON

VOCABULARY: Selection Vocabulary (continued)

5. At first the cubs stay near their mother, but soon they will _____ out on their own.

Ⓐ clutch   Ⓑ signal

Ⓒ venture   Ⓓ shun

6. The kitten climbed too high and was _____ at the top of the tree.

Ⓐ cashed   Ⓑ stranded

Ⓒ repaired   Ⓓ bid

7. Some birds _____ know to fly south for the winter.

Ⓐ foolishly   Ⓑ wishfully

Ⓒ loosely   Ⓓ instinctively

8. The glass vase is _____ and will break easily if you drop it.

Ⓐ fragile   Ⓑ confident

Ⓒ serious   Ⓓ patient

Harcourt • Reading Skills Assessment

GO ON

Touch a Dream / Theme 2

VOCABULARY: Selection Vocabulary (continued)

9. The long drive was _____, so we went straight to bed when we got home.

(A) fresh (B) exhausting

(C) supported (D) feasting

10. Do not laugh when my brother acts silly or you might _____ him to act silly again.

(A) encourage (B) earn

(C) catch (D) range

11. I am sorry to say that I felt _____ when my friend got a new bike.

(A) rhymed (B) coiled

(C) crowded (D) jealous

12. As the _____ began telling the story, the actors made their way onto the stage.

(A) restaurant (B) absence

(C) narrator (D) puzzle

GO ON

VOCABULARY: Selection Vocabulary (continued)

13. I can tell from your _____ expression that you are happy today.
- (A) tall
- (B) loud
- (C) grooved
- (D) facial

14. Some animals are thought of as _____ because there are so few of them left.
- (A) visited
- (B) worked
- (C) endangered
- (D) covered

15. We looked forward to the class party with eager _____ .
- (A) anticipation
- (B) investigation
- (C) worries
- (D) chores

16. We saw no one around, so we decided that the island was _____ .
- (A) uninhabited
- (B) educated
- (C) listened
- (D) behaved

GO ON

VOCABULARY: Selection Vocabulary (continued)

17. On some days my hair won't do anything I like, but on other days it
is more _____ .

(A) returnable (B) manageable

(C) excitable (D) drinkable

18. The dog showed his _____ by knocking over his water dish.

(A) rescue (B) displeasure

(C) lesson (D) survival

19. To play ball well you need to have good hand-eye _____ .

(A) disappointment (B) questions

(C) coordination (D) celebration

20. The plants were _____ into the country, even though they might
carry harmful insects.

(A) rested (B) smuggled

(C) reminded (D) sounded

STOP

COMPREHENSION: Predict Outcomes

Directions: Read each passage. Fill in the answer circle in front of the correct answer for each question.

Jared and his dad were camping out near a lake. They were sleeping in sleeping bags inside a large tent. Very early one morning Jared got up, picked up a spade and a tin can, went outside the tent, and began to dig up worms to use as bait. When he had quite a few worms in the can, he grabbed his fishing pole.

"If we want to catch anything to cook for breakfast, we'd better get going, Jared," his dad said.

"I'm ready!" Jared answered. "I hope the fish are as hungry as I am!"

21. What are Jared and his dad most likely to do now?
- Ⓐ hike up a mountain
- Ⓑ fish in the nearby lake
- Ⓒ take down their tent
- Ⓓ get into their sleeping bags

22. What will Jared and Dad probably eat for breakfast?
- Ⓐ pancakes
- Ⓑ bacon
- Ⓒ fish
- Ⓓ cereal

GO ON

Touch a Dream / Theme 2

COMPREHENSION: Predict Outcomes (continued)

At school, Kerry's social studies class is studying about the pyramids in Egypt. The teacher gives each student a homework assignment. After school, Kerry goes to the public library, finds the section of the library that has sets of encyclopedia, and takes Volume *P* from the shelf. He opens the encyclopedia, reads for a while, and takes some notes on what he has read. Then he puts the book back on the shelf.

23. What will Kerry most likely do with the notes he took?

Ⓐ throw them away

Ⓑ give them to a friend

Ⓒ use them to write a report

Ⓓ use them to cover a textbook

24. What will Kerry probably do in social studies class tomorrow?

Ⓐ give a talk on pyramids to his class

Ⓑ ask where the public library is

Ⓒ explain how to take notes

Ⓓ ask his teacher for a different assignment

STOP

COMPREHENSION: Cause and Effect

Directions: Read each passage. Fill in the answer circle in front of the correct answer for each question.

Jess did an experiment to find out the effects of light on green plants. First, he got six small plants that looked the same in every way. Next, he put two of the plants near a sunny window, two in a dark closet, and two on a table in the hallway that did not get much light. He watered the plants as needed. At the end of three weeks, he checked the plants and found that the two plants that had been near the sunny window were much taller than before, and they looked healthy. The plants on the table were alive, but they looked pale and hadn't grown much. The two plants in the closet had died.

25. The plants in the closet probably died because they _____ .
Ⓐ got too much water
Ⓑ had bad soil
Ⓒ did not get enough light
Ⓓ were eaten by bugs

26. Why is Jess most likely to put plants near the window from now on?
Ⓐ The soil in the plant pots needs to get fresh air.
Ⓑ Plants need sunlight to grow and stay healthy.
Ⓒ Plants put there will need less water.
Ⓓ Flowers will look better near the window.

GO ON ▶

Touch a Dream / Theme 2

COMPREHENSION: Cause and Effect (continued)

   Sand is made up of loose grains of minerals or rocks. Most grains of sand are parts of solid rocks that have crumbled away. Rocks can become broken down in several ways. Some rocks crumble because they are affected by air, rain, or frost. Strong waves beating against rocks can also break them down.

   Sand appears in many places on Earth. It can be found at the bottom of the sea, shallow lakes, or rivers. Great amounts of sand are found on beaches. In deserts, sand can cover hundreds of miles. It is often piled up by the wind in hills called sand *dunes*.

27. The passage says that rocks break down into sand because _____ .
    Ⓐ machines grind the rocks
    Ⓑ air, rain, frost, or waves affect the rocks
    Ⓒ fires turn the rocks into ash
    Ⓓ people crush the rocks by walking on them

28. Why do sand dunes form in the desert?
    Ⓐ Wind blows the sand into hills.
    Ⓑ Rain makes the sand stick together in clumps.
    Ⓒ Heat causes some parts to expand.
    Ⓓ Pressure underground forces the sand up.

STOP

Side by Side / Theme 2
Reading Skills Assessment

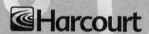

Orlando   Boston   Dallas   Chicago   San Diego

Part No. 9997-06742-8

ISBN 0-15-314464-5 (Package of 12)

Reading Skills Assessment

Touch a Dream / Theme 3

Name _____ Date _____

SKILL AREA	Criterion Score	Pupil Score	Pupil Strength
VOCABULARY Selection Vocabulary	9/12	_____	_____
COMPREHENSION Draw Conclusions	3/4	_____	_____
Sequence	3/4	_____	_____
Compare and Contrast	3/4	_____	_____
TOTAL SCORE	18/24	_____	_____

Were accommodations made in administering this test?   ☐ Yes   ☐ No

Type of accommodations: _____

_____

ISBN 0-15-314464-5

1 2 3 4 5 6 7 8 9 10 170 2003 2002 2001 2000

VOCABULARY: Selection Vocabulary

> **Directions:** Read each sentence. Fill in the answer circle in front of the word that best completes each sentence.

1. The shivering puppy seemed to be _____ by the loud thunder.
   - Ⓐ hungered
   - Ⓑ alarmed
   - Ⓒ wanted
   - Ⓓ tasted

2. We could hear the soft _____ of the leaves in the trees.
   - Ⓐ rustle
   - Ⓑ business
   - Ⓒ practice
   - Ⓓ respect

3. I would understand my lessons better if I had someone to _____ me.
   - Ⓐ travel
   - Ⓑ bloom
   - Ⓒ tutor
   - Ⓓ harvest

4. It upsets me to hear you and your sister _____ with each other.
   - Ⓐ bicker
   - Ⓑ collect
   - Ⓒ arrange
   - Ⓓ plant

GO ON

VOCABULARY: Selection Vocabulary (continued)

5. We tried to calm my aunt, who is a very _____ person.

   Ⓐ metal   Ⓑ excitable

   Ⓒ chewable   Ⓓ frozen

6. Our plan was approved because it is clear and _____ .

   Ⓐ thorny   Ⓑ sickly

   Ⓒ logical   Ⓓ backward

7. We hoped the other team would give up, or _____ .

   Ⓐ surrender   Ⓑ create

   Ⓒ spend   Ⓓ instruct

8. As soon as the rain _____, we can go outside to play.

   Ⓐ expresses   Ⓑ collapses

   Ⓒ reaches   Ⓓ ceases

GO ON

VOCABULARY: Selection Vocabulary (continued)

9. We have an _____ supply of food, so we won't go hungry.
Ⓐ answered   Ⓑ abundant
Ⓒ ill   Ⓓ empty

10. When we spend time together, my baby brother and I are _____ .
Ⓐ bonding   Ⓑ melting
Ⓒ drizzling   Ⓓ stinging

11. The rain forest is a natural _____ for many plants and animals.
Ⓐ harness   Ⓑ habitat
Ⓒ toll   Ⓓ sport

12. Once a plant dies, it _____ very quickly.
Ⓐ denies   Ⓑ decomposes
Ⓒ deserves   Ⓓ dances

STOP

COMPREHENSION: Draw Conclusions

Directions: Read the passage. Fill in the answer circle in front of the correct answer for each question.

I found a raccoon last spring during a camping trip. I took it home and fed it warm milk through a straw. Now it weighs more than fifteen pounds, and it eats everything. Mr. Brown, our neighbor, has said, "Bob, if your raccoon gets in my garden one more time, I'll make a coonskin cap out of him!" Eating isn't the only problem. My sister was really upset when my raccoon hid her gold ring in its nest.

It is spring again, and my raccoon seems restless. We ride slowly up the river in my canoe. We hear the sound of another raccoon on the shore. My raccoon answers with a soft call. Suddenly, it dives into the water and swims toward the sound. I wait for a long, long time. Finally, I turn the canoe around and paddle slowly home.

GO ON

COMPREHENSION: Draw Conclusions (continued)

13. The raccoon that Bob found was probably from _____.
    - (A) the wild
    - (B) a pet shop
    - (C) the circus
    - (D) a zoo

14. What word would Mr. Brown and Bob's sister use to describe the raccoon?
    - (A) adorable
    - (B) playful
    - (C) silly
    - (D) bothersome

15. Bob's raccoon jumped out of the boat because it wanted to _____.
    - (A) drink some water
    - (B) swim to Bob's house
    - (C) join the other raccoon
    - (D) play a game with Bob

16. At the end of the story, Bob most likely felt _____.
    - (A) sad
    - (B) angry
    - (C) shy
    - (D) happy

STOP

COMPREHENSION: Sequence

Directions: Read the passage. Fill in the answer circle in front of the correct answer for each question.

It is easy to make blueberry muffins using a box mix. First, get together all the things you will need: an egg, water, muffin tins, baking spray, strainer, can opener, small mixing bowl, and a large spoon.

Second, preheat the oven to 400°.

Third, put baking spray into each muffin cup to keep the muffins from sticking.

Next, open the can of blueberries that comes in the mix. Pour the berries into a strainer and rinse them with water.

Then put one egg and 3/4 cup of water into the mixing bowl. Blend together with the spoon. Then add the muffin mix and stir until the egg, water, and mix are smooth.

After that, add the strained blueberries to the batter and mix them in with the spoon. Then spoon the batter into the greased muffin cups. Fill each cup about 3/4 full. Then bake about 20 minutes or until golden brown. Last, let the muffins cool about 5 minutes before serving them.

GO ON

COMPREHENSION: Sequence (continued)

17. What do you do **first** to make these blueberry muffins?
- Ⓐ Preheat the oven.
- Ⓑ Open the can of blueberries.
- Ⓒ Get together the things you will need.
- Ⓓ Put the egg and water into a bowl.

18. What do you do **right after** you mix in the blueberries?
- Ⓐ Blend the egg and water together with the spoon.
- Ⓑ Put baking spray into each muffin cup.
- Ⓒ Pour the berries into a strainer.
- Ⓓ Spoon the batter into the muffin cups.

19. What do you do **just before** baking the muffins?
- Ⓐ Put the egg and water into the mixing bowl.
- Ⓑ Fill each muffin cup about 3/4 full.
- Ⓒ Open the can of blueberries that comes in the mix.
- Ⓓ Put baking spray into each muffin cup.

20. What is the **last** step before serving the muffins?
- Ⓐ Let the muffins cool about 5 minutes.
- Ⓑ Stir the egg, water, and mix until smooth.
- Ⓒ Rinse the berries with water.
- Ⓓ Add the strained berries to the batter.

STOP

COMPREHENSION: Compare and Contrast

> **Directions:** Read the passage. Fill in the answer circle in front of the correct answer for each question.

Lions and tigers are the largest animals in the cat family. Some people say the tiger is fiercer than the lion, but the lion is still thought to be among the strongest and fiercest of all wild creatures.

The bodies of tigers and lions are similar, but they can look quite different. A lion's coat can vary from buff yellow, orange-brown, or silver gray to dark brown. Male lions usually have a mane, which may be short or long and light or dark. Tigers are known for their striped markings. Depending on the type of tiger and the place where it lives, a tiger's coat may be bright reddish tan with dark stripes, or it may be paler or black and white. The tiger has no mane.

Both lions and tigers are meat eaters, and they usually hunt at night. They prefer to prey upon medium- to large-size animals such as zebras and antelopes, but they have been known to attack much larger animals.

Lions are unique among cats in that they live and hunt in a group, or *pride*. A pride is made up of several generations of lionesses (female lions), their cubs, and one or two adult male lions. Tigers usually live alone.

GO ON

Harcourt • Reading Skills Assessment

COMPREHENSION: Compare and Contrast (continued)

21. According to this passage, both tigers and lions can be described

as _____ .

Ⓐ fierce

Ⓑ quiet

Ⓒ tame

Ⓓ friendly

22. One way that tigers and lions are the same is that they both _____ .

Ⓐ have bright reddish tan fur

Ⓑ have manes

Ⓒ are members of the cat family

Ⓓ live in prides

23. The coat of a tiger is different from the coat of a lion because the tiger's

coat has _____ .

Ⓐ spots

Ⓑ thicker fur

Ⓒ longer fur

Ⓓ striped markings

24. One way tigers are different from lions is that tigers usually _____ .

Ⓐ hunt at night

Ⓑ live alone

Ⓒ eat meat

Ⓓ attack antelopes

STOP

Harcourt • Reading Skills Assessment

Make Yourself at Home / Theme 3
Reading Skills Assessment

Harcourt

Orlando   Boston   Dallas   Chicago   San Diego

Part No. 9997-06743-6

ISBN 0-15-314464-5 (Package of 12)

Reading Skills Assessment

Touch a Dream / Theme 4

Name _____ Date _____

SKILL AREA	Criterion Score	Pupil Score	Pupil Strength
VOCABULARY Selection Vocabulary	15/20	_____	_____
COMPREHENSION Main Idea and Details	6/8	_____	_____
Summarize and Paraphrase	3/4	_____	_____
TOTAL SCORE	24/32	_____	_____

Were accommodations made in administering this test? ❏ Yes ❏ No

Type of accommodations: _____

_____

ISBN 0-15-314464-5

1 2 3 4 5 6 7 8 9 10 170 2003 2002 2001 2000

VOCABULARY: Selection Vocabulary

Directions: Read each sentence. Fill in the answer circle in front of the word that best completes each sentence.

1. Tom invented a _____ that helps people open jars easily.
   - (A) delay
   - (B) hurdle
   - (C) device
   - (D) castle

2. We might need to _____ our plan since we now have less money to spend.
   - (A) remain
   - (B) admire
   - (C) modify
   - (D) amuse

3. Eat this nice, _____ bowl of soup to give you energy.
   - (A) strengthening
   - (B) molding
   - (C) juggling
   - (D) asking

4. He is _____ with his money, always putting some aside for the future.
   - (A) faint
   - (B) rash
   - (C) thrifty
   - (D) confused

GO ON

VOCABULARY: Selection Vocabulary (continued)

5. Because I was so hungry, Mother gave me a _____ piece of the pie.
   Ⓐ rude   Ⓑ generous
   Ⓒ developed   Ⓓ gentle

6. I have always been _____ by animals, and I love to be near them.
   Ⓐ remarked   Ⓑ faulted
   Ⓒ fascinated   Ⓓ galloped

7. I learned my lines for the play by reading the _____ over and over.
   Ⓐ chance   Ⓑ substitute
   Ⓒ comfort   Ⓓ script

8. You have done me a serious _____ by saying that I did something wrong.
   Ⓐ injustice   Ⓑ instant
   Ⓒ sketch   Ⓓ weave

GO ON

Touch a Dream / Theme 4

VOCABULARY: Selection Vocabulary (continued)

9. My friend _____ the newspaper as soon as she finishes
   reading it.
   Ⓐ wanders   Ⓑ discards
   Ⓒ disables   Ⓓ rebuilds

10. We should probably stay home, under the _____ .
    Ⓐ circumstances   Ⓑ contents
    Ⓒ structures   Ⓓ sections

11. The king _____ that taxes should be paid throughout the land.
    Ⓐ wrapped   Ⓑ decreed
    Ⓒ wrinkled   Ⓓ stalked

12. In times of _____, many people go hungry.
    Ⓐ posture   Ⓑ direction
    Ⓒ famine   Ⓓ detail

GO ON

VOCABULARY: Selection Vocabulary (continued)

13. The student received top honors for both athletic ability
and _____ .
Ⓐ companion   Ⓑ relationship
Ⓒ scholarship   Ⓓ return

14. "I guess you think you're smart," she _____ .
Ⓐ retorted   Ⓑ accepted
Ⓒ tossed   Ⓓ repacked

15. We fastened the two ends of the paper together to make
a _____ headband.
Ⓐ lost   Ⓑ furious
Ⓒ flooded   Ⓓ circular

16. I knew _____ that I would like you.
Ⓐ straightaway   Ⓑ questioningly
Ⓒ confusingly   Ⓓ getaway

GO ON

VOCABULARY: Selection Vocabulary (continued)

17. Burt could not be guilty because he had an _____ for the time of the crime.

(A) energy   (B) amount

(C) alibi   (D) instrument

18. "Someone, please help me!" the woman cried out _____ .

(A) desperately   (B) secretly

(C) safely   (D) tamely

19. The king's subjects _____ him to lower their taxes.

(A) gained   (B) implored

(C) answered   (D) invented

20. We will eat here often if we find the food _____ .

(A) accidental   (B) emotional

(C) acceptable   (D) breakable

STOP

COMPREHENSION: Main Idea and Details

Directions: Read each passage. Fill in the answer circle in front of the correct answer for each question.

Air pollution has become a problem in many parts of our country today. When harmful substances end up in the air and make it unhealthy for us to breathe, we say that the air has become *polluted*.

Most air pollution results from human activities, but *pollutants* (substances that make the air unhealthy) can come from natural sources, too. A volcano, for example, can give off clouds of matter and gas that can harm living things. Dust storms and smoke from forest fires also pollute the air. Other natural pollutants include such things as pollen and bacteria.

Much of the manmade pollution in our country comes from vehicles, such as cars, trucks, buses, and airplanes. Other sources of manmade pollution are factories, power plants, furnaces, and the burning of garbage and other wastes.

Air pollution can be harmful to both humans and animals. It can lead to breathing difficulties and other health problems for both young and old.

GO ON

COMPREHENSION: Main Idea and Details (continued)

21. What is the main idea of this passage?

Ⓐ A volcano can give off clouds of matter and gas that can harm living things.

Ⓑ Air pollution has become a problem in many parts of our country today.

Ⓒ Other sources of manmade pollution are factories, power plants, furnaces, and the burning of garbage.

Ⓓ Other natural pollutants include such things as dust, pollen, and bacteria.

22. Which of these is a source of manmade pollution?

Ⓐ televisions

Ⓑ books

Ⓒ medicines

Ⓓ trucks

23. Which of these is a source of natural pollution?

Ⓐ whales

Ⓑ volcanoes

Ⓒ rocks

Ⓓ stars

24. According to the passage, air pollution can lead to _____ .

Ⓐ health problems

Ⓑ forest fires

Ⓒ dust storms

Ⓓ bacteria growth

GO ON

COMPREHENSION: Main Idea and Details (continued)

Railroads played an important part in helping the ranching industry in Texas to grow. In the early 1800s, there was not a lot of money to be made from raising cattle in Texas. Ranchers at that time raised cattle mostly for leather and for fat, which they used to make candles and soap. Later, people in cities in the East became eager to buy beef, and they were willing to pay a lot of money to get it. Ranchers could get ten times as much money for their cattle in the East as they could get in Texas. However, they had no good way to get the cattle from Texas to the cities in the East.

Railroads helped the ranchers by providing a way to get Texas cattle to distant markets. Ranchers began to organize cattle drives along trails that led from Texas through Oklahoma and north to "cow towns." The cow towns were places where *stockyards*, or cattle pens, were built near railroad lines. When the herds reached the stockyards, they could be loaded into railroad cars. The railroad cars could then carry the beef to markets in the East.

COMPREHENSION: Main Idea and Details (continued)

25. What is this passage mostly about?

Ⓐ how to build and operate a railroad

Ⓑ how railroads helped Texas cattle ranchers

Ⓒ future plans for railroads in Texas

Ⓓ how to make candles and soap from beef fat

26. Ranchers wanted to sell their cattle in the East because _____ .

Ⓐ people in the East would pay more for beef

Ⓑ no one in Texas would buy beef

Ⓒ in Texas, beef could only be used to make leather

Ⓓ they wanted to help the railroads make money

27. Ranchers organized cattle drives to _____ .

Ⓐ move cattle to warmer places for the winter

Ⓑ bring new breeds of cattle from the East back to Texas

Ⓒ get their cattle to stockyards near railroads

Ⓓ keep cattle moving so they could not be stolen

28. Cow towns were important to ranchers because the cow towns _____ .

Ⓐ had cattle pens built near railroads

Ⓑ were all located in the East

Ⓒ had the best grazing land for cattle

Ⓓ were the best place to get supplies for cattle drives

STOP

COMPREHENSION: Summarize and Paraphrase

Directions: Read each passage. Fill in the answer circle in front of the correct answer for each question.

The Garza family had many things to do today. The weekend of the family picnic had finally arrived, and it was to be held in their backyard.

Carlos had to trim the bushes and mow the yard so that his younger brother, Joe, could arrange the tables and set up the folding chairs. Dad was cleaning the large barbecue grill and before long would start the fire. Mom had been cooking since dawn, with Delores and Frankie as her assistants. Will, the youngest, spent his time licking cake batter from the mixing bowls.

The morning was warm, and Joe's muscles ached. He wondered whether a family gathering was worth all this effort. Then he remembered that his grandmother always said that no matter what happens in life, you will always have your family to fall back on. He smiled at the memory and went back to work.

GO ON

COMPREHENSION: Summarize and Paraphrase (continued)

29. What is the best summary of this passage?

Ⓐ Joe remembered his grandmother saying that no matter what happens in life, you will always have your family to fall back on.

Ⓑ The men in the family did jobs like trimming bushes, mowing the yard, setting up tables, and cleaning the grill, while the women did the cooking.

Ⓒ The Garza family had many things to do to get ready for the family picnic, and Carlos, Joe, Dad, Mom, Delores, Frankie, and Will each had a job to do. Joe wondered if a family gathering was worth so much effort, but he decided it was.

Ⓓ The weekend of the family picnic had finally arrived. Everyone was excited about spending time together eating, telling stories, and playing games.

30. Which statement is the best paraphrase of this passage?

Ⓐ The Garzas had many things to do to prepare for an important family event.

Ⓑ Carlos had to trim the bushes and mow the lawn.

Ⓒ Mom had been cooking for days, aided by Delores, Frankie, and Will.

Ⓓ The morning was warm, and Joe's muscles ached.

GO ON

COMPREHENSION: Summarize and Paraphrase (continued)

Miranda's family was enjoying one last summer outing before school started—a day of hiking in the nearby mountains. As Miranda followed her family down the last leg of the trail, she slipped on a loose rock and fell with her left arm beneath her. She knew her wrist was hurt but didn't realize it was broken until her mother screamed. When they reached their car, they made a beeline for the closest hospital.

Before Miranda knew it, her arm was covered in an ugly cast. She was unhappy about starting fifth grade wearing a cast, but she decided to make the cast prettier by drawing colorful designs on it and by letting her family and friends write on it. "Now, that's better," Miranda thought.

---

31. Which of the following is the best summary of this passage?

Ⓐ While hiking with her family, Miranda slipped, broke her wrist, and had to wear a cast. She was unhappy about starting fifth grade in a cast until she decided to let her family and friends write on it.

Ⓑ Miranda's family had planned one last summer outing—a day of hiking in the nearby mountains.

Ⓒ Miranda hurt her wrist but did not know it was broken until her mother screamed.

Ⓓ Miranda was unhappy about starting fifth grade with a cast on her arm.

32. Which statement is the best paraphrase of this passage?

Ⓐ Miranda had become a little bored with summer vacation.

Ⓑ Miranda didn't realize her wrist was broken at first.

Ⓒ Miranda broke her wrist but made the best of wearing a cast.

Ⓓ Miranda and her family went hiking in the mountains.

STOP

Harcourt • Reading Skills Assessment

Creative Minds / Theme 4
Reading Skills Assessment

Orlando   Boston   Dallas   Chicago   San Diego

Part No. 9997-06749-5

ISBN 0-15-314464-5 (Package of 12)

4

Reading Skills Assessment

Touch a Dream / Theme 5

Name _____ Date _____

SKILL AREA	Criterion Score	Pupil Score	Pupil Strength
VOCABULARY Selection Vocabulary	9/12	_____	_____
COMPREHENSION Fact and Opinion	3/4	_____	_____
Author's Purpose and Perspective	3/4	_____	_____
STUDY AND RESEARCH SKILLS Locating Information (Book Parts)	6/8	_____	_____
TOTAL SCORE	21/28	_____	

Were accommodations made in administering this test? ❏ Yes ❏ No

Type of accommodations: _____

_____

VOCABULARY: Selection Vocabulary

Directions: Read each sentence. Fill in the answer circle in front of the word that best completes each sentence.

1. Those oil-soaked rags are highly _____ and should not be put near a fire.
   - Ⓐ flammable
   - Ⓑ thinkable
   - Ⓒ rattled
   - Ⓓ hiked

2. His _____ to the team is beyond question.
   - Ⓐ current
   - Ⓑ dedication
   - Ⓒ body
   - Ⓓ lantern

3. My friend _____ to me for breaking my pencil.
   - Ⓐ floated
   - Ⓑ drifted
   - Ⓒ awaited
   - Ⓓ apologized

4. We asked the students to help decorate the room, and they happily _____ .
   - Ⓐ wasted
   - Ⓑ splashed
   - Ⓒ obliged
   - Ⓓ tracked

GO ON

VOCABULARY: Selection Vocabulary (continued)

5. We loved to dance along to the music my uncle played on
   the _____ .
   Ⓐ privilege   Ⓑ accordion
   Ⓒ decoration   Ⓓ costume

6. When she did not get her way, she would go _____ to her room
   to pout.
   Ⓐ joyously   Ⓑ smoothly
   Ⓒ sulkily   Ⓓ meltingly

7. A large lump _____ from his forehead where the ball had hit him.
   Ⓐ protruded   Ⓑ guarded
   Ⓒ closed   Ⓓ respected

8. I could tell by his medals that he was _____ a brave soldier.
   Ⓐ undoubtedly   Ⓑ swimmingly
   Ⓒ hurriedly   Ⓓ funnily

GO ON

Harcourt • Reading Skills Assessment

VOCABULARY: Selection Vocabulary (continued)

9. In class, we are studying the _____ of the ancient Egyptians.
Ⓐ breath   Ⓑ fins
Ⓒ culture   Ⓓ senses

10. At the party, we threw _____ and got it in our hair!
Ⓐ clouds   Ⓑ confetti
Ⓒ mist   Ⓓ mysteries

11. We play basketball every Friday night in the school _____.
Ⓐ mountain   Ⓑ certificate
Ⓒ document   Ⓓ gymnasium

12. My parents set a _____ for my older brother so that he will come home at a certain time.
Ⓐ curfew   Ⓑ photograph
Ⓒ dictionary   Ⓓ relative

STOP

COMPREHENSION: Fact and Opinion

Directions: Read the passage. Fill in the answer circle in front of the correct answer for each question.

Most people hate skunks. That is because skunks give off an unpleasant odor. Skunks are members of the weasel family. Weasels are unpopular animals, also. It is not surprising to learn that skunks and weasels are in the same family.

Skunks are strange-looking animals. They are about the size of a large house cat, and they have black and white markings. The white fur on a skunk's forehead and back look exactly as if someone painted a stripe right down its back. The skunk has an arched back, a broad forehead, and short legs. It moves rather slowly. A skunk looks silly when it walks.

A skunk has a pair of glands near its tail. When a skunk is frightened, these glands can give out a bad-smelling fluid to help defend it from its enemies. A skunk can shoot the fluid as far as ten feet into the air. The glands can be removed, and then skunks make the best pets in the world. Everyone should have a pet skunk at least once!

Skunks sleep during the day and come out at night. All farmers love skunks. This is because skunks eat insects, rats, mice, and other small animals that can hurt crops. Skunks also eat eggs, though, so they are not so helpful to farmers raising hens.

GO ON

Touch a Dream / Theme 5

COMPREHENSION: Fact and Opinion (continued)

13. Which of the following is a **fact** from the passage?

Ⓐ Most people hate skunks.

Ⓑ Weasels are unpopular animals.

Ⓒ It is not surprising to learn that skunks and weasels are in the same family.

Ⓓ The skunk has an arched back, a broad forehead, and short legs.

14. Which of the following is an **opinion** from the passage?

Ⓐ Skunks sleep during the day and come out at night.

Ⓑ Skunks make the best pets in the world.

Ⓒ Skunks eat insects, rats, mice, and other small animals.

Ⓓ Skunks also eat eggs.

15. Which of the following is a **fact** from the passage?

Ⓐ Everyone should have a pet skunk at least once!

Ⓑ A skunk looks silly when it walks.

Ⓒ Skunks are members of the weasel family.

Ⓓ All farmers love skunks.

16. Which of the following is an **opinion** from the passage?

Ⓐ Skunks have black and white markings.

Ⓑ A skunk has a pair of glands near its tail.

Ⓒ The glands can be removed.

Ⓓ Skunks are strange-looking animals.

STOP

COMPREHENSION: Author's Purpose and Perspective

Directions: Read each passage. Fill in the answer circle in front of the correct answer for each question.

Author 1

The Statue of Liberty is a large statue that stands in New York Harbor. France gave the statue to the United States in 1884 as a symbol of friendship and of the freedom that citizens enjoy under our form of government.

The statue shows a proud woman dressed in a loose robe. Her right arm holds a great torch raised high in the air. Her left arm holds a tablet bearing the date of the Declaration of Independence. On her head is a crown of spikes, like huge rays of the sun. At her feet is a broken shackle, which stands for the overthrowing of tyranny.

At the base of the statue is a poem, "The New Colossus," written by Emma Lazarus. The poem tells how the Statue of Liberty welcomes immigrants to America.

Author 2

There are many wonderful sights to see in New York, but there is only one sight that you really must see—the Statue of Liberty. It is one of the most beautiful sights in the world. So many times I have heard my grandmother tell about the first time she saw the statue when she and her family came to the United States to live. She said she knew that it meant they were welcome in America—land of the free.

The statue has welcomed many, many immigrants to our country. To people who may have left their homelands because of war, hunger, or fear, the statue is a symbol of hope, freedom, and a new chance at a good life. This is why you really must go to see the Statue of Liberty.

GO ON

COMPREHENSION: Author's Purpose and Perspective (continued)

17. The main purpose of Author 1 is to _____ .

(A) persuade   (B) inform

(C) entertain   (D) warn

18. Which of the following statements would most likely be used by Author 1?

(A) The Statue of Liberty is the most beautiful sight in the entire world.

(B) The Statue of Liberty stands 151 feet high and weighs about 450,000 pounds.

(C) No other sight in America could ever mean as much to visitors as the Statue of Liberty.

(D) The Statue of Liberty rises tall and proud and must never be removed because it is a symbol of hope for so many.

19. The main purpose of Author 2 is to _____ .

(A) persuade   (B) inform

(C) entertain   (D) warn

20. Which of the following statements would most likely be used by Author 2?

(A) The Statue of Liberty stands for all the hopes and dreams of people who first come to America.

(B) The Statue of Liberty serves no purpose but looks pretty.

(C) The Statue of Liberty should be moved out of New York Harbor.

(D) The Statue of Liberty costs too much to maintain and should be taken down.

STOP

STUDY AND RESEARCH SKILLS: Locating Information

Directions: Fill in the answer circle in front of the correct answer for each question.

21. Where should you look to find out when a book was published?
  - Ⓐ the table of contents
  - Ⓑ the copyright page
  - Ⓒ the index
  - Ⓓ the glossary

22. Where should you look to find biographical information about the author of a book?
  - Ⓐ the book jacket
  - Ⓑ the title page
  - Ⓒ the copyright page
  - Ⓓ the table of contents

23. Becky wants to know whether her social studies textbook has any information on the Great Plains. Where should she look to see whether this topic is in the book?
  - Ⓐ the cover
  - Ⓑ the title page
  - Ⓒ the index
  - Ⓓ the glossary

24. Hector does not know the meaning of a specialized term in his science book. Where should he look to find out the meaning of the word?
  - Ⓐ the book jacket
  - Ⓑ the table of contents
  - Ⓒ the index
  - Ⓓ the glossary

GO ON

Harcourt • Reading Skills Assessment

STUDY AND RESEARCH SKILLS: Locating Information (continued)

Contents

Atlas A1

Globes and World Maps 4

Chapter 1

LESSON 1 • A Nation of Immigrants 8

LESSON 2 • Our Country's Resources 22

LESSON 3 • Waterways of America 46

LESSON 4 • Industry in the United States 68

Chapter 2

25. In which lesson should you look to find information about people who moved from Poland to settle in the United States?
    (A) Globes and World Maps
    (B) A Nation of Immigrants
    (C) Waterways of America
    (D) Industry in the United States

26. In which lesson should you look to find information about steel mills in the United States?
    (A) Globes and World Maps
    (B) A Nation of Immigrants
    (C) Waterways of America
    (D) Industry in the United States

GO ON

STUDY AND RESEARCH SKILLS: Locating Information (continued)

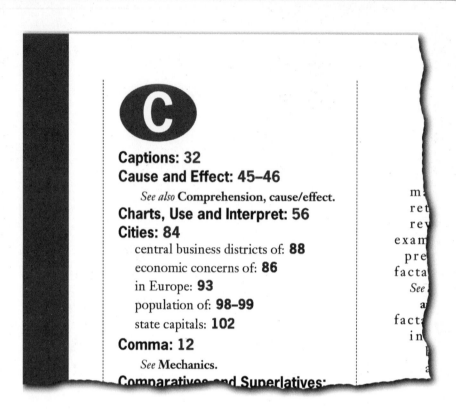

27. Where should you look to find information about the population
of a large city in Maryland?

Ⓐ page 86

Ⓑ page 88

Ⓒ pages 98–99

Ⓓ page 102

28. Where should you look to find information about the capital
of Utah?

Ⓐ page 86

Ⓑ page 88

Ⓒ pages 98–99

Ⓓ page 102

STOP

Score _____

Touch a Dream / Theme 5

Harcourt • Reading Skills Assessment

COLLECTIONS

Community Ties / Theme 5

Reading Skills Assessment

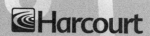

Orlando   Boston   Dallas   Chicago   San Diego

Part No. 9997-06750-9

ISBN 0-15-314464-5 (Package of 12)

sessment

heme 6

Name _____ Date _____

SKILL AREA	Criterion Score	Pupil Score	Pupil Strength
VOCABULARY			
Selection Vocabulary	12/16	_____	_____
Vocabulary in Context	6/8	_____	_____
STUDY AND RESEARCH SKILLS			
Graphic Sources	6/8	_____	_____
TOTAL SCORE	24/32	_____	_____

Were accommodations made in administering this test?   ❑ Yes   ❑ No

Type of accommodations: _____

_____

Printed in the United States of America

ISBN 0-15-314464-5

1 2 3 4 5 6 7 8 9 10 170 2003 2002 2001 2000

Harcourt • Reading Skills Assessment

VOCABULARY: Selection Vocabulary

Directions: Read each sentence. Fill in the answer circle in front of the word that best completes each sentence.

1. You can be anything you want to be; the _____ are endless.
   - Ⓐ excuses
   - Ⓑ patients
   - Ⓒ possibilities
   - Ⓓ celebrations

2. The soldier ate his _____ of food for the day.
   - Ⓐ altitude
   - Ⓑ ration
   - Ⓒ network
   - Ⓓ years

3. The inventor had all kinds of interesting _____ in his workshop.
   - Ⓐ rescues
   - Ⓑ phases
   - Ⓒ winds
   - Ⓓ gadgets

4. We need an _____ to help us understand the foreign language.
   - Ⓐ alarm
   - Ⓑ existence
   - Ⓒ amateur
   - Ⓓ interpreter

GO ON ▶

Harcourt • Reading Skills Assessment

VOCABULARY: Selection Vocabulary (continued)

5. The fans were screaming _____ at the end of the game.
- (A) silently
- (B) quietly
- (C) hysterically
- (D) gracefully

6. Those little sandwiches on the tray look _____ .
- (A) whispered
- (B) appetizing
- (C) hopeful
- (D) serious

7. As we walked, I _____ reached down to pet my dog.
- (A) invisibly
- (B) noisily
- (C) occasionally
- (D) dizzily

8. The butterwort eats insects, so it is a _____ plant.
- (A) youthful
- (B) nervous
- (C) sincere
- (D) carnivorous

GO ON

Touch a Dream / Theme 6

VOCABULARY: Selection Vocabulary (continued)

9. My cake tasted bad because I _____ mixed in salt instead of sugar.

   Ⓐ highly   Ⓑ accidentally

   Ⓒ wholly   Ⓓ weakly

10. The spider will catch a _____ in its web.

   Ⓐ victim   Ⓑ hike

   Ⓒ plaster   Ⓓ legend

11. We _____ our cafeteria into a beautiful garden by using flowers and foil to decorate.

   Ⓐ trickled   Ⓑ transformed

   Ⓒ puzzled   Ⓓ breathed

12. Mr. Clark will _____ to solve the mystery for us.

   Ⓐ investigate   Ⓑ empty

   Ⓒ ooze   Ⓓ fasten

GO ON

VOCABULARY: Selection Vocabulary (continued)

13. That is the mother wolf, and these are her pups, _____ .

Ⓐ lowly   Ⓑ apparently

Ⓒ daintily   Ⓓ carefully

14. We tried not to make noise as we tiptoed along the long _____ .

Ⓐ friction   Ⓑ century

Ⓒ sample   Ⓓ corridor

15. An early _____ in America most likely had to grow his vegetables and hunt for his meat.

Ⓐ pioneer   Ⓑ monument

Ⓒ statue   Ⓓ fabric

16. The two sisters sing in perfect _____ .

Ⓐ harmony   Ⓑ carelessness

Ⓒ capitals   Ⓓ denials

STOP

Score _____

Touch a Dream / Theme 6

Harcourt • Reading Skills Assessment

VOCABULARY: Vocabulary in Context

> **Directions:** Read each passage. Fill in the answer circle in front of the correct answer for each question.

The score in our baseball game was tied. On the last play of the game, I was playing outfield when a fly ball came toward me. I really tried to catch it, but I dropped the ball. The umpire called it an <u>error</u>, and the other team scored. Later, in the players' locker room, I could hear the <u>tread</u> of sneakers coming toward me. I recognized our coach's familiar walk. What would he say to me about causing us to lose the game?

17. The word <u>error</u> in this passage means _____ .
  Ⓐ wrong measure
  Ⓑ misplay in baseball
  Ⓒ mistake or accident
  Ⓓ false belief

18. The word <u>tread</u> in this passage means _____ .
  Ⓐ hurt someone's feelings
  Ⓑ grooves on a tire
  Ⓒ step or walk
  Ⓓ staying upright in water

GO ON ▶

VOCABULARY: Vocabulary in Context (continued)

Mel <u>resembled</u> his twin brother Seth so much that they looked almost exactly the same.

"It is just <u>incredible</u> how much you two boys look alike," their neighbor said. "I mean, it is just hard to believe that two people could look so much alike in every way."

19. The word <u>resembled</u> in this passage means _____ .

Ⓐ tricked

Ⓑ disliked

Ⓒ amused

Ⓓ looked like

20. The word <u>incredible</u> in this passage means _____ .

Ⓐ unbelievable

Ⓑ annoying

Ⓒ tempting

Ⓓ honorable

GO ON

VOCABULARY: Vocabulary in Context (continued)

Feeling butterflies in her stomach, Janice laid her notes on the podium and put her hands on the sides of the wooden stand so the audience couldn't see her hands or papers shaking. She knew if she forgot the poem she was to recite to the class, she would be ridiculed and laughed at for days. She did her best to breathe deeply and think only about the poem—not how many people were listening.

21. The word podium in this passage means _____ .
   Ⓐ low wall
   Ⓑ stand for a speaker
   Ⓒ foot-shaped object
   Ⓓ script

22. The word ridiculed in this passage means _____ .
   Ⓐ angry
   Ⓑ rhymed words
   Ⓒ made fun of
   Ⓓ breathed fast

GO ON

VOCABULARY: Vocabulary in Context (continued)

Tony was totally <u>engrossed</u> in his book. The story was so interesting and his attention was so focused on what he was reading that he didn't even hear the bell ring. An <u>exodus</u> of students out of the classroom began, but Tony stayed in his seat, reading. Finally, his teacher said, "Tony, I'm so happy you're enjoying your book, but don't you think you should get to your next class?"

23. The word <u>engrossed</u> in this passage means _____ .

Ⓐ copied by hand

Ⓑ interested or engaged

Ⓒ bought in large amounts

Ⓓ stuck to

24. The word <u>exodus</u> in this passage means _____ .

Ⓐ loud noise

Ⓑ mass exit

Ⓒ sitting position

Ⓓ strong liking

STOP

Score _____

STUDY AND RESEARCH SKILLS: Graphic Sources

> **Directions:** Look at the graph and the chart that follow. Then read the questions that follow the graph or chart. Fill in the answer circle in front of the correct answer for each question.

The World's Top Five Rice-Producing Countries in 1997–98

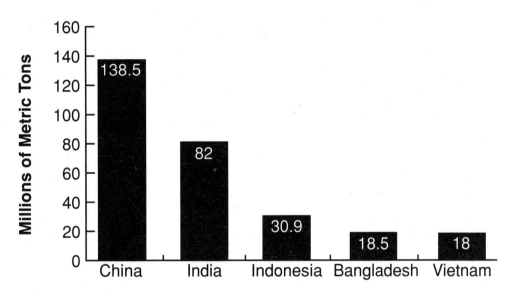

25. Which country produced the **most** rice?

Ⓐ China   Ⓑ India

Ⓒ Bangladesh   Ⓓ Vietnam

26. Which country produced the **least** rice?

Ⓐ China   Ⓑ India

Ⓒ Bangladesh   Ⓓ Vietnam

27. Which country produced **almost the same** amount of rice as Vietnam produced?

Ⓐ China   Ⓑ India

Ⓒ Indonesia   Ⓓ Bangladesh

GO ON ▶

STUDY AND RESEARCH SKILLS: Graphic Sources (continued)

Population History of Ten United States Cities from 1850–1900 (in thousands)						
	1850	1860	1870	1880	1890	1900
Atlanta	3	10	22	37	66	90
Boston	137	178	251	363	448	560
Chicago	30	109	299	503	1,100	1,698
Detroit	21	46	80	116	206	286
Houston	3	5	9	17	26	45
Los Angeles	2	4	6	11	50	102
Memphis	9	3	10	34	64	103
New York	696	1,175	1,478	1,912	2,507	3,437
Philadelphia	121	566	674	847	1,049	1,293
San Francisco	35	57	149	234	299	343

28. Which city had the **lowest** population **in 1880**?

Ⓐ Los Angeles
Ⓑ New York
Ⓒ Philadelphia
Ⓓ San Francisco

29. Which city had the **greatest** population **in 1880**?

Ⓐ Los Angeles
Ⓑ New York
Ⓒ Philadelphia
Ⓓ San Francisco

GO ON

Touch a Dream / Theme 6

Harcourt • Reading Skills Assessment

STUDY AND RESEARCH SKILLS: Graphic Sources (continued)

30. Which two cities had **almost the same** population **in 1900?**
    Ⓐ Los Angeles and Mempis
    Ⓑ Boston and Chicago
    Ⓒ Atlanta and Detroit
    Ⓓ Philadelphia and San Francisco

31. Which city's population **doubled between 1850 and 1860?**
    Ⓐ Atlanta
    Ⓑ Houston
    Ⓒ Los Angeles
    Ⓓ Memphis

32. Which city's population **got smaller between 1850 and 1860?**
    Ⓐ Atlanta
    Ⓑ Chicago
    Ⓒ Detroit
    Ⓓ Memphis

STOP

Collections

New Lands / Theme 6
Reading Skills Assessment

Harcourt

Orlando   Boston   Dallas   Chicago   San Diego

Part No. 9997-06751-7

ISBN 0-15-314464-5 (Package of 12)